DATE DUE RENEWALS 691-4574

Demco, Inc. 38-293

WHO WILL DO SCIENCE?

Who Will Do Science?
Educating the Next Generation

EDITED BY

Willie Pearson, Jr., and Alan Fechter

The Johns Hopkins University Press
Baltimore and London

THE JOHNS HOPKINS UNIVERSITY PRESS
2715 NORTH CHARLES STREET
BALTIMORE, MARYLAND 21218-4319
THE JOHNS HOPKINS PRESS LTD., LONDON

ISBN 0-8018-4857-1

Library of Congress Cataloging-in-Publication Data will be found at the end of this book.

A catalog record for this book is available from the British Library.

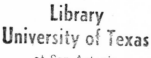

TO

LaDessa E. Pearson (Spelman '95)
and Avram Fechter
WHO REPRESENT THE HOPE AND PROMISE OF
AMERICA'S NEXT GENERATION OF TALENT

Contents

List of Illustrations   ix

List of Tables   xi

Foreword, by Linda S. Wilson   xiii

Preface   xv

Acknowledgments   xxi

CHAPTER 1   1
The Next Generation of Scientists and Engineers:
Who's in the Pipeline? *Betty M. Vetter*

CHAPTER 2   20
Investing in Human Potential: Policies and Programs
in Higher Education. *Marsha Lakes Matyas*

CHAPTER 3   43
Barriers to Women's Participation in Academic Science
and Engineering. *Henry Etzkowitz, Carol Kemelgor,
Michael Neuschatz, and Brian Uzzi*

CHAPTER 4   68
The Contributions of Historically Black Colleges and
Universities to the Production of African American Scientists
and Engineers. *William Trent and John Hill*

CHAPTER 5   81
Bachelor's Degree Chemists, 1970–1990: Past Choices and
Future Prospects. *Terrence Russell*

CHAPTER 6   96
    Trends in Science and Engineering Doctorate Production,
    1975–1990. *Earl Smith and Joyce Tang*

CHAPTER 7   125
    Future Supply and Demand: Cloudy Crystal Balls. *Alan Fechter*

CHAPTER 8   141
    Human Resources in Science and Engineering:
    Policy Implications. *Cheryl B. Leggon and Shirley M. Malcom*

    References   153
    Contributors   167

Illustrations

1.1 Percentage of college freshmen with plans to major in science and engineering fields, 1966–1992   2

1.2 Effect of taking high school geometry on going to college, high school class of 1982   4

1.3 Trends in mathematics proficiency by race/ethnicity and grade, 1990   8

1.4 International math test, age 13: percentage correct, 1991   10

1.5 Trends in science proficiency by race/ethnicity and age, 1970–1990   13

1.6 Percentage of women graduates with bachelor's in science and engineering, 1960–1991   16

1.7 Percentage of women graduates, 1991   18

4.1 Bachelor's degrees earned by African Americans in historically black colleges and universities, 1977, 1981, 1989   73

4.2 Bachelor's degrees earned by African Americans in traditionally white colleges and universities, 1977, 1981, 1989   74

5.1 Chemistry degrees as a proportion of all bachelor's degrees, 1970–1988   83

5.2 Bachelor's degrees awarded in chemistry, 1970–1988   84

5.3 Annual percentage shares of bachelor's degrees in chemistry, 1970–1988   86

5.4 Bachelor's degrees in chemistry awarded by 104 predominantly black institutions, 1970–1989   87

5.5 Further education plans of graduates with B.S. degrees, 1989   88

5.6 Salaries of chemists with B.S. degrees as a percentage of salaries of chemists with Ph.D.'s, 1975–1989   90

5.7 Professional age shifts, 1975–1989   91

5.8 Chemists with B.S. degrees working in analytical or environ-   92
    mental chemistry

5.9 Work function by years since receiving the B.S. degree, 1975–   93
    1989

7.1 Supply and demand projections for all arts and sciences, model 2   132

Tables

1.1 Percentage of high school students taking mathematics courses   5
by graduation, 1982 and 1990

2.1 Target groups for intervention programs, by program type   30

4.1 Percentage and number of African American bachelor's degree   75
recipients in science and engineering fields from historically
black colleges and universities, 1989

4.2 Percentage and number of African American master's degree   77
recipients in science and engineering fields from historically
black colleges and universities, 1989

4.3 Overview of the role of historically black colleges and universi-   78
ties among African Americans in conferral of science and engineering degrees, by level, 1989

5.1 Bachelor's degree recipients in chemistry by race/ethnicity   85
(%), 1975–1989

6.1 Doctorates in science and engineering awarded to U.S. citizens,   98
by gender, race/ethnicity, and field, 1975–1990

6.2 Educational background of parents of doctorates in science and   100
engineering, 1975–1990

6.3 Source of support of doctorates in science and engineering with   102
U.S. citizenship, by gender and race/ethnicity, 1975–1990

6.4 Median number of years to doctoral degree for U.S. citizens,   104
by gender, race/ethnicity, and field, 1975–1990

6.5 Postgraduation plans of doctorates with U.S. citizenship, by   108
gender and race/ethnicity, 1975–1990

6.6 Employment rates for doctoral scientists and engineers with   110
U.S. citizenship, by gender, race/ethnicity, and field, 1989

6.7   Full-Time employed doctoral scientists and engineers, by gen-   112
      der, race/ethnicity, and sector, 1989

6.8   Academically full-time employed doctoral scientists and engi-   115
      neers, by gender, race/ethnicity, rank, and field, 1989

6.9   Tenured doctoral faculty, by rank and field, 1989   116

6.10 Median annual salaries of full-time employed doctoral scien-   118
      tists and engineers, by gender, race/ethnicity, field, and sector,
      1989

6.11 Earnings ratios of full-time employed doctoral scientists and   120
      engineers, by gender, race/ethnicity, field, and sector, 1989

Foreword

Human resource inputs are a critical component to our scientific enterprise. We look to scientists for creative sparks to expand our knowledge base and deepen our understanding of natural and social phenomena. Their contributions provide the basis for technological advances that improve our productivity and the quality of lives. It is not surprising, therefore, that concern about the adequacy of this talent pool, both in numbers and quality, is a hardy perennial that appears regularly as an important policy issue.

The issue of adequacy in numbers has always been the subject of strong, and sometimes heated, debate. A long training period is required to acquire an entry-level degree for research and innovation in the sciences (usually a doctorate). And this produces alternative cycles of boom and bust that result in periods of overproduction and underproduction of scientific talent. We have not progressed significantly in our ability to anticipate and assess our national needs for these skills. Moreover, we have a long way to go in deepening our understanding of career choice, the factors associated with this choice, and how these factors operate to influence this choice. For these reasons, our estimates of future labor market conditions for scientists are both unreliable and imprecise.

Given the uncertainties outlined above and the current condition of weak job opportunities in many fields, I do not know whether we will experience overall shortages in the future. I do know, however, that we currently face real shortages of talent from underrepresented groups— women and racial/ethnic minorities—and that we will continue to face these talent deficits in the foreseeable future. Failure to utilize these pools of talent to their maximum potential imposes costs not only on our scientific enterprise, but on society as a whole.

Unfortunately, we are not making satisfactory progress in understanding how to reduce this deficit. The issues involved are complex. They include the motives of students as they consider alternative careers, the overall health of the economy, the political process of allocating public funds for science and science training, and many others. Given this complexity, progress in assessing adequacy and in reducing the talent deficit among underrepresented groups will require contributions from a broad array of disciplines.

This book represents an important first step in attempting to meet this need. The issues examined are important. The emphasis is on achieving diversity in our talent pool of scientists; the sources that provide this diversity; and the barriers confronted in acquiring the requisite training and in successfully pursuing careers.

A statistical overview reveals a steadily improving rate of participation in science for women and non-Asian minorities; but it also indicates we have a long way to go before we achieve rates that will eliminate underutilization of these important talent pools. Given projections that these talent pools will grow in relative importance as potential sources of supply, this conclusion is extremely important. It implies the need for programs that will effectively improve both recruitment and retention of these groups, both while they are in training and during their careers.

The chapters of this volume forthrightly address these issues. One study describes recruitment and retention programs to expand these talent pools and discusses the effectiveness of the programs. It reveals that there are gaps in our efforts, that some programs work, and that our ability to assess and evaluate program effectiveness is extremely limited. Another, an ethnographic study, describes barriers facing female graduate students and faculty. One chapter examines the role of historically black institutions in developing African American scientists. Another chapter examines the talent pool of chemists, focusing on the bachelor's degree. Still another concentrates on doctorates and covers all science fields. The issue of future supply and demand is addressed by a critical evaluation of two widely cited projections studies. A final chapter draws policy implications from the findings of the earlier chapters.

The findings highlight what we know and—perhaps more importantly—what we do not know. The studies featured in this book will stimulate others to invest time and effort in the worthy cause of improving our understanding of this highly complex set of issues.

                                         Linda S. Wilson
                                         President, Radcliffe College

Preface

Issues of adequacy and equity have long been major components of the human resource policy agenda. These issues are especially compelling for our talent pool of scientists. Concerns about possible shortage have recently been dramatically transformed into concerns that we may be overproducing. The debate has focused on the validity of projected shortages of scientists and engineers with little regard for the issue of composition—the ability of the current system to diversify its talent pool. Diversity of the science and engineering talent pool is also a significant issue, however, regardless of the state of the labor market. A combination of demographic changes and declines in student interest in science and technical careers continues to feed the concern about the future pool of scientific talent. This book explores the dimensions of that concern. It also fashions policy responses to the stubborn trends and uncertainties that dominate such markets in dynamic economies. Above all, this book is about real people, not just aggregate statistics. It explores the development of talent among our citizens.

Two important demographic changes affect our ability to produce the next generation of scientists and engineers: trends in the annual number of births and the increasingly diverse racial or ethnic backgrounds of those born. Today, half of all high school graduates are women; and one in four is a racial/ethnic minority. Traditionally, both of these groups (especially African Americans and Hispanics) have underparticipated in science and engineering.

The possible effect of these demographic trends on both the level and the diversity of our scientific talent pool is exacerbated by trends in career interests of students. Fewer high quality students are choosing careers in science and engineering. The percentage of Merit Scholars choosing science and engineering majors has fallen from 43 in 1983 to 35 in 1988. Among students scoring above the 90th percentile on the mathematics portion of the Scholastic Aptitude Test (SAT), the percentage planning science and engineering majors dropped from 44 in 1982 to 38 in 1991. Over the past two decades, the interest of college freshmen in science or engineering majors has dropped by nearly half. Of those academically able students entering college with intentions to major in science, fully half switch to nonscience majors (Green, 1989). Concern has also been expressed about the adequacy of the science and math training of our student population, as measured by performance of American students on science and mathematics achievement tests, both nationally and internationally.

One consequence of these trends is that a significant and increasing proportion of graduate students are foreign citizens. The implications of these trends are not clear. In the past, we have counted as benefits the contributions made to our domestic talent pool by those who remain in the United States. But the value of this contribution becomes more problematic in today's environment of possible excess supply. And there remains the question of the relative absence of Americans—particularly those from underrepresented groups—in these graduate programs, although recent increases in both graduate enrollment and degree production are encouraging signs.

The net result of these trends is that fewer Americans may be available at a time when more job openings are expected. The large numbers of academic scientists and engineers hired in the 1950s and 1960s will soon reach retirement age. At the same time, the number of students reaching college age will be increasing.

Despite the current perceptions of overproduction, the confluence of these expected supply and demand changes suggests that attracting talented students into the sciences and engineering will remain a key policy issue. This elevates the importance of devising ways to tap more deeply into underutilized talent pools in order to meet future needs. A recent Office of Technology Assessment (OTA) report (U.S. Congress, 1991) points out that equal opportunity for participation in higher education and in research for all citizens is a long-term social goal achievable only with persistent and consistent national commitment and investments. The report suggests that programs targeted to U.S. minorities, women, and the disabled could help to expand the pool of potential scientists and engineers.

Concerns about the aforementioned trends motivated a group of distinguished scholars from a range of disciplines to examine issues related to the prospective flow of student talent through the science and engineering pipeline and, ultimately, to the workplace. The results of their investigations are presented here. In Chapter 1, Betty M. Vetter provides a backdrop, a portrait of students in higher education. Her analysis suggests that the pipeline is unprepared to provide a continuous stream of students qualified to choose science and engineering majors when more are needed. Not only is the number of students graduating from high school the lowest in a quarter century, but the proportion qualified to elect science and engineering fields has grown smaller. Vetter argues that any attempt to in-

crease the science and engineering talent pool must take into account ra-
cial/ethnic minorities and women. Her findings point to a low, albeit
improving, participation rate among women and non-Asian minorities in
science, and especially in engineering.

In Chapter 2, Marsha Lakes Matyas reports on efforts to expand the
science and engineering talent pool. Her analysis focuses on programs and
services currently in operation at U.S. colleges and universities designed to
recruit and retain underrepresented groups such as women, minorities, and
persons with disabilities in science and engineering careers at the precollege, college, graduate, and faculty levels. Matyas also discusses the effectiveness of these programs in attaining their various goals. She points out
that evaluation must be an integral component of intervention programs
and not merely "add-ons" at the programs' completion. Specific program
goals should be established and evaluation methods designed to assess
those goals. Program staff must be involved in each aspect of the evaluation in order to make it a productive effort that informs program design
and operation. For Matyas, creating an atmosphere that promotes diversity
among the science and engineering faculty and the student body requires
focusing on policies and programs both in academic and social life.

In Chapter 3, Henry Etzkowitz, Carol Kemelgor, Michael Neuschatz,
and Brian Uzzi examine the structural and cultural barriers and covert
resistance by male (and some female) faculty that hinder the participation
of women in the physical sciences and engineering in academe. The authors contribute to our understanding of these issues by reporting on experiences of women faculty members and graduate students at two research
universities. They conclude that after successfully negotiating the numerous barriers to scientific and technical careers, many women often pursue
less demanding careers than their male peers. They argue that the organization and culture of academic science deter many women from making
their contribution to science and technology. The authors report that, in
those instances when a department altered its policies and practices,
women's participation improved dramatically. They argue that even if
changes in institutional policies do not change attitudes, they can affect
behavior. From their analysis, the authors suggest ways in which women's
participation in science and engineering may be further enriched. They
conclude that federal policy has a major role to play in this effort.

Historically black colleges and universities (HBCUs) have traditionally
served as a conduit for the production of African American scientists and
engineers. William Trent and John Hill's discussion in Chapter 4 examines
the contribution these institutions make to the production of African
American scientists and engineers. The authors focus on the fields in which
HBCUs play a prominent role, at both the undergraduate and the graduate

levels. Their analysis reveals that HBCUs are a vital national resource in the production of African American scientists and engineers, especially at the baccalaureate level. Because HBCUs have not traditionally had the resources and support to build the foundations of graduate research programs, their graduate degree production has declined in recent years.

The science and engineering talent pool is also an important source of supply of scientific and technical personnel for chemical and other related industries. In Chapter 5, Terrence Russell describes the past and present status of those with such degrees in chemistry. Baccalaureates in chemistry are a significant source of U.S. chemistry Ph.D.'s and M.D.'s. Russell also examines the mobility of this highly diverse group. Finally, his analysis of the future prospects of bachelor's-degree chemists addresses demographic change and occupational choice (especially for women and minorities), labor market demands in an increasing variety of industries, and the implications for demand of the rising complexity and sophistication of technology. Russell argues that in the 1990s, the B.S. degree will become the basic requirement for entry into technical industrial jobs. This will intensify the problem of declining numbers of B.S. graduates unless ways are found to bring the required technical skill and training to the workplace.

A growing proportion of the science and engineering doctorate pool is comprised of women, Asian Americans, and foreign-born individuals. In Chapter 6, Earl Smith and Joyce Tang describe the changing demographic profile of science and engineering doctorate recipients and examine trends by race or ethnicity to field in these areas: the time it takes to earn the degree, postgraduation plans, and financial support. They report that non-Asian minorities and women continue to be underrepresented at the highest levels of science and engineering education. However, women have made greater gains than non-Asian minorities. Among minorities, African Americans had the smallest growth in doctoral degree recipients. The degree of field segregation between whites and minorities as well as between males and females is more pronounced in work than in training. The authors suggest that the increasing presence of foreign scientists and engineers may adversely affect the production of minority and women doctorates.

In Chapter 7, Alan Fechter reviews and evaluates selected studies that examine whether the future supply of Ph.D. scientists will be adequate to meet the United States's future workplace needs. He assesses two widely cited projection models, emphasizing the uncertainty associated with forecasts of supply and demand. He concludes that these models tend to overstate potential shortages. He discusses mechanisms that can bring supply and demand into balance and examines the resource implications associated with their use, claiming that some mechanisms may produce socially undesirable side effects—particularly for underrepresented minorities. Fechter also addresses decision making in the face of the uncertainties associated with such models. He states his preference for a strategy that tilts toward anticipating shortages, arguing that the costs of being wrong in this case would be preferable to the cost of tilting toward an erroneous assumption that markets will eventually be in balance. He advocates close monitoring of and comparison between actual experiences and projections. He argues that such efforts will enable policy analysts to make midcourse corrections in projections and in policy implications, if such corrections are deemed necessary.

In the final chapter, Cheryl B. Leggon and Shirley M. Malcom draw on the substantive findings of the previous chapters. They present guidelines for the development of effective science policy strategies. Leggon and Malcom conclude that market forces alone cannot increase the size and diversity of the science and engineering work force in the United States. It is further argued that systematic reform need not—perhaps cannot—occur at once, but must be incremental over time. They conclude that a carefully crafted human resource policy, informed by systematic data collection and analysis, and combined with flexible programs and practices, will generate the institutional changes necessary to increase the size and diversity of the U.S. science and engineering work force.

Sound policy decisions concerning the recruitment, support, training, and utilization of scientific and engineering personnel require knowledge about the factors affecting the choice of careers, and the impact, both quantitatively and qualitatively, of these choices on the health of the labor market for scientists and engineers. We hope that the work presented in this volume will provide a basis for informing such decisions.

Acknowledgments

From the beginning this has been a truly collaborative effort, not only by the editors and contributors, but by colleagues who have volunteered their time to read various drafts of the manuscripts. Without the assistance of these individuals, the project would have been much more difficult to complete. Their collective energies and encouragement have made this project an enriching and intellectually rewarding experience.

Special thanks are due to the members of our editorial review board: Bernice T. Anderson (Educational Testing Service); Beatriz C. Clewell (Educational Testing Service); Eugene H. Cota-Robles (University of California at Santa Cruz); Harriet G. Jenkins (U.S. Senate); Melvin Thompson (Howard University); Samuel L. Myers, Jr. (University of Minnesota); Isiah Warner (Louisiana State University); Jerry Gaston (Texas A and M University); Shirley Vining Brown (Educational Testing Service); Howard Tuckman (Virginia Commonwealth University); Harriet Zuckerman (Columbia University and the Mellon Foundation); Yolanda S. George (American Association for the Advancement of Science); J. Scott Long (Indiana University); Michael Feuer (National Academy of Sciences); Howard Garrison (Federation of American Societies for Experimental Biology); Cora B. Marrett (National Science Foundation); Sue Kemnitzer (National Science Foundation); John R. Earle (Wake Forest University); and David G. Brown (Wake Forest University).

Special recognition is due to Daryl Chubin (National Science Foundation).

The project benefited enormously from the administrative assistance of Cathy Jackson at the Office of Scientific and Engineering Personnel and Susan King of Wake Forest University. Both played a major role in administering the external review process and serving as the liaison between chapter writers and reviewers. We are grateful to Cathy and Susan for their patience and managerial skills.

To Jacqueline Wehmueller, our editor at the Johns Hopkins University Press, we are especially indebted. She convinced the editors of the importance and timeliness of the subject of this volume. And she challenged the editors and the authors to dig deeply within themselves to produce the best work possible.

The development of human resources was also a vital part of this project. Thus, a number of former Wake Forest University undergraduates made substantial contributions to the project. Among these are Frances Reeves, Catherine A. Mayes, Nichola L. Marshall, Laura A. Baliles, Lesley R. Williams, Gloria E. Lindsey, Africa Dalton, Jennifer E. Grishkin, and Tiffini K. Williamson.

This publication was supported, in part, by grants from the Wake Forest University Research and Publication Fund and the National Science Foundation (INT-9220282 and SBR-9222547).

The views expressed in this volume are those of the authors; they do not necessarily reflect those of their institutions or agencies. Finally, the editors assume full responsibility for any errors that remain.

CHAPTER 1

The Next Generation of Scientists and Engineers: Who's in the Pipeline?

Betty M. Vetter

As we move through the final decade of the century, a combination of demographic changes and declines in student interest in scientific and technical careers challenges us to better reflect the talent of an increasingly diverse population and, simultaneously, to assure our ability to meet national needs. Two important demographic changes affect our ability to produce the next generation of scientists and engineers: the trends in the annual number of births and the increasingly diverse racial and ethnic backgrounds of those who have been born.

The annual number of births dropped 25 percent from 1956 to 1976. As a consequence of this trend, the annual number of high school graduates dropped from 3.1 million in 1977 to 2.4 million in 1992. Beginning in 1977, the annual number of births began to rise again, and thus in 1993, the number of high school graduates also started slowly upward again.

More than half of current high school graduates are women, and one of every four is a member of a minority group—each non-Asian group distinguished by its disproportionately low representation in science and engineering. The profile of the student population will continue to become increasingly Hispanic, African American, and Asian American. Thus, our ability to maintain adequate interest in science and engineering will become increasingly difficult without involving more women and more minorities. More importantly, if we do not expand the base population from which to draw interested students to science and engineering, we will lose an increasing fraction of the talent available to us.

The effect of these demographic trends on degree production in science and engineering fields is further exacerbated by trends in career interests of students. Figure 1.1 shows a shrinking proportion of both male and female college freshmen who indicate plans to major in one of these fields (Astin et al., 1991).

Of equal or greater concern are indications that top quality students are

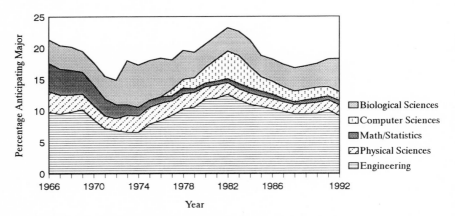

Figure 1.1. Percentage of college freshmen with plans to major in science and engineering fields, 1966–1992. Values for 1986, 1987, and 1989 are estimated based on linear interpolation.

Sources: 1966–85: Astin, Green, and Korn, 1987, pp. 90, 93; *1988:* Astin et al., 1988, pp. 53–54; *1990:* Astin, Korn, and Berz, 1990, pp. 50–51; *1991:* Astin et al., 1991, pp. 20–21; *1992:* Astin et al., 1992.

opting out of science and engineering. Among National Merit Scholars, the share choosing majors in the natural sciences or engineering dropped from 43 percent in 1983 to 35 percent in 1988 (National Science Board, 1989a). Among students scoring above the 90th percentile on the math Scholastic Aptitude Test, the percentage planning majors in natural science or engineering has dropped from 44 percent in 1982 to 38 percent in 1991 (National Science Board, 1991). The decrease is slightly larger for women than for men.

A consequence of these trends has been a declining number of baccalaureate graduates in natural science and engineering fields beginning in 1987. The trend in freshman plans assures a continued drop, at least through 1996.

Concerns about these trends motivated the development of this book. The individual chapters that follow examine a variety of issues related to the educational system and its role in meeting the future human resource requirements of our science and technology enterprise. This chapter provides a factual background to support these examinations.

Precollege Level

Factors that affect precollege education are basic to understanding the production of new scientists and engineers. Unless we understand the entire education spectrum, from preschool through graduate school, we cannot target intervention strategies in an optimum manner—at the right place and the right time—in that education continuum we sometimes call the pipeline. Actually, "pipeline" is not the best metaphor to describe the process by which students drop out of science or stay in. Some students who lose interest in science in early school years renew that interest later and return to take more courses in science. But much of the flow through this porous "pipeline" is outward, particularly for female and minority youth.

Both schools and society display a distinct bias against girls that particularly discourages their participation in science. There is "compelling evidence that girls are not receiving the same quality, or even quantity, of education as their brothers" (American Association of University Women, 1992), according to one study of how girls are disadvantaged in America's schools. In relation to science and mathematics, "as young women 'learn' that they are not good at these topics, their sense of self-worth and aspirations for themselves deteriorate," according to another large study of the critical changes in attitudes and identity among girls and boys by the American Association of University Women (1991). By the time they reach high school, girls have lost a major part of their self-esteem. This loss continues throughout their adolescent years, while boys begin to achieve more confidence in themselves as they move through high school.

Although we are unaware of any comparable studies for racial or ethnic minorities, a similar bias exists against those groups. Exemplary schools where disadvantaged children excel in mathematics or in other areas because of an outstanding teacher or principal are often in the news.[1] Equally demonstrable is the fact that, when they are believed to be less competent, minority students fulfill that expectation.

Mathematics

A strong foundation in mathematics is an essential ticket for admission to and success in science and engineering careers. Inadequate preparation restricts career choices and results in exclusion from science and engineering fields. Half of all American students drop out of math classes by ninth grade, and we lose half of the remaining students in math each year from grade nine to the Ph.D. (National Research Council, 1989a).

Coursework

Although some states increased the number of math credits required for graduation during the 1980s, most did not specify which math courses should be taken. One response has been for students to take more courses in general or consumer math, which do little to advance their knowledge of mathematics.

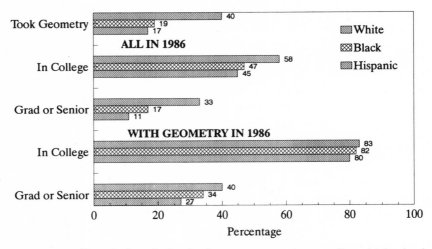

Figure 1.2. Effect of taking high school geometry on going to college, high school class of 1982.

Source: College Board. Graph by CPST.

A study conducted for the College Board (Pelavin and Associates, 1990) found that taking geometry in high school is a major predictor of both college attendance and college success and that racial differences in college attendance and persistence essentially disappear among students taking this level of mathematics (see fig. 1.2). Typically, students taking geometry had first taken a year of algebra.

Recent data from the 1990 mathematics assessment by the National Assessment of Educational Progress (NAEP) confirm the results of earlier studies that the level of mathematics reached in high school is strongly related to student achievement in mathematics. Data in the 1990 NAEP on mathematics courses taken by twelfth grade students showed significant increases in mathematics proficiency scores with each additional course. For example, students who did not take algebra had an average scale score of 266; those who had completed algebra 1 averaged 286; those who had completed algebra 2 scored 309; and students who had taken a fourth level of mathematics averaged 327. The same pattern of increases related to course enrollment held for students in all racial/ethnic and socioeconomic (SES) groups (Mullis et al., 1991, pp. 126–27).

Sex differences in course enrollments decreased during the eighties, and by 1990, participation by girls and boys was about the same through sec-

Table 1.1. Percentage of High School Students Taking Mathematics
Courses by Graduation, 1982 and 1990

	1982	1990	Change (%)
Algebra 1			
Asian American	66	72	6
Black	57	78	21
Hispanic	55	81	26
White	68	77	9
Algebra 2			
Asian American	56	59	3
Black	24	39	15
Hispanic	21	39	18
White	39	52	13
Calculus (regular & AP) *			
Asian American	19	34	15
Black	2	4	2
Hispanic	2	7	5
White	8	11	3

Source: Westat, Inc., 1993.
* Advanced placement.

ond-year algebra, or third-level mathematics. At the level of calculus, an average of 6 percent more boys were enrolled than girls. Changes in mathematics enrollments among minorities from 1982 to 1990 were large, but a significant gap remains in taking courses beyond algebra 1 (see table 1.1).

Achievement

The National Assessment of Educational Progress, established in the late sixties to measure achievement levels of American students over time, administers tests in various fields to a typical sample of American students who are 9, 13, and 17 years old. Each subject is tested every few years.

Female students scored only slightly below males in the 1986 mathematics assessment. Scores are identical at age 9, similar at age 13, and only slightly below at age 17—a difference that appears to be related to courses taken. Nonetheless, the conventional wisdom mistakenly states that boys are better at math than girls. This erroneous information is transmitted to girls at an early age, convincing many of them that anything they do not understand immediately must be beyond their capacity to understand.

The latest NAEP assessment of mathematical achievement, combined for most of the states in 1992, finds that, as in 1990, American eighth graders across the nation have not mastered more than basic arithmetic (Mullis et al., 1993). American youth show weakness in complex reasoning and problem solving skills.[2] The 1990 report notes that students are ill-equipped to cope confidently with the mathematical demands of today's society, such as the graphs in the media and the regulations and procedures that underlie credit cards, discounts, taxes, insurance, and benefit plans (Mullis et al., 1991).[3]

Scoring was on a scale from 0 to 500. A panel of mathematics educators see level 200 as material typically covered by the third grade, level 250 as material covered by the fifth grade, level 300 as content introduced by the seventh grade, and level 350 as content generally covered in high school mathematics courses in preparation for the study of advanced mathematics. Overall, twelfth graders averaged 295, eighth graders, 265, and fourth graders, 216, all well below the levels that should be expected of students in those grades. More than half of twelfth graders scored below the 300 level expected of eighth graders, and only 5 percent scored 350 or better, the achievement level expected for their grade. These top scorers were described as "equipped to do college work" in advanced algebra and geometry, but "not necessarily calculus."

There were notable gender and racial/ethnic differences in achievement. By grade eight, the proportion of boys who demonstrated less than basic competence was greater than the proportion of girls at that level, but there also were more boys than girls at the proficient level. These patterns were more pronounced at grade twelve.

Girls are less likely than boys to be encouraged by teachers and especially counselors to enroll in the "hard" math sequence required to prepare a high school student to be able to choose a science or engineering career. Even girls who are mathematically gifted are less likely to be selected by their teachers and principals than similarly qualified boys for special programs such as the University of Minnesota's Talented Youth Mathematics Program (Keynes, 1991), and those who are selected and enter the program are less likely than boys to be encouraged to continue in it by parents, peers, and teachers. Half of all elementary school boys but only one-third of girls say they are good at math. By high school, one in four males but only one in seven females say they are good in math (American Association of University Women, 1991).

The effects of course taking are dramatically illustrated by a recent study (Adelman, 1991). Although women score below men on the mathematical sections of college entrance and other tests, women from the high school class of 1972 who studied more than two years each of mathematics and science in high school performed as well as men with the same course background on the SAT and ACT. Those who chose to enter engineering and science in college earned better grades than their male classmates and were more likely to continue into graduate school. But they had less confidence in their ability to do mathematics than did the men in the class, even though they consistently earned higher grades than did their male classmates, who felt more self-confident about their mathematical abilities.

Minority differences in math scores on the NAEP assessments are substantial. African American and Hispanic children already are well behind white children by age 9,[4] and despite steady improvement in minority scores from 1978 to 1986, while white scores scarcely moved (Dossey et al., 1988), the achievement gap was still a major problem in 1990 and again two years later (Mullis et al., 1991, 1993).

More than half of Native American, Hispanic, and African American students were below basic mathematics achievement levels (see fig. 1.3), and less than 10 percent of the minority students ranked at or above the proficient level. Asian American students, on the other hand, score solidly above white students. Only about one-fifth of all students were proficient—that is, able to do solid work at their grade level (Borque and Garrison, 1991).

America tolerates underachievement in mathematics because of the common belief that mathematical ability is innate in certain people, most of whom will be male. In many other industrialized countries, however, all students are expected to master a level of mathematical understanding equivalent to that attained by only our best students (Mullis et al., 1991).

American students rank poorly in mathematics achievement when compared to students in other countries. Achievement levels of American 13-year-olds were compared with 12-year-olds in Japan and Hong Kong and 13-year-olds in eighteen other countries in 1986 (Lapointe, Mead, and Phillips, 1989). American students ranked last in this comparison. Additionally, American twelfth graders who were enrolled in advanced college-preparatory mathematics courses were compared with a similar age group in the same countries.

American students have shorter school days and a shorter school year, and they test well below the students of other countries. In calculus, our very best math students scored near the achievement level of the average students in other countries. Our precalculus college-prep students scored substantially below the international average, and their scores were the lowest of the advanced countries.[5]

These 1986 international scores are not available by sex. However, a more recent 1988 international math test for 13-year-olds still found the United States at the bottom of the scoring, with the girls' scores lagging slightly behind the boys' (National Science Board, 1989). Cross-national studies of sex differences in mathematics suggest that "differences in mathematics performance are predominantly due to the accumulated effects of sex-role stereotypes in family, school and society" (National Research Council, 1989a).

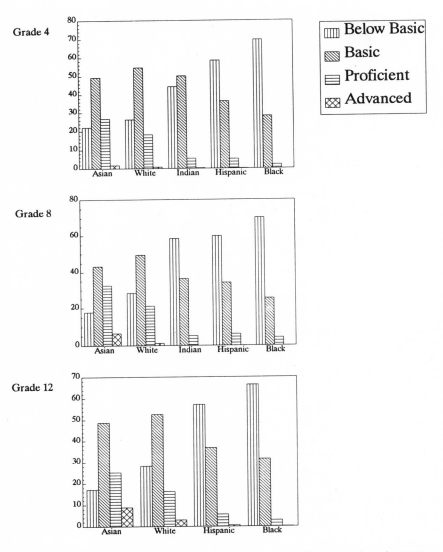

Figure 1.3. Trends in mathematics proficiency by race/ethnicity and grade, 1990. Data not available for Native Americans for grade 12.

Source: NAEP. Graph by CPST.

Another international assessment in 1991 compared 9- and 13-year-old students in the United States with those in other countries. Once again, Americans ranked lowest in almost every category (Center for the Assessment of Educational Progress, 1992a, 1992b), confirming beyond any doubt the accuracy of earlier studies that showed great deficiencies in the science and mathematics education of American students. Ironically, the study was undertaken and funded by the National Science Foundation and the U.S. Department of Education's National Center for Education Statistics in response to critics who questioned the reliability and validity of results from earlier international studies. This new study incorporated procedures designed to clarify differences in school enrollment rates between the participating countries, and it collected new information about student and school practices to explain differences in achievement.

At age 9, American students are already far behind in math, ranking near the bottom in giving correct answers among a world of students. In science, U.S. 9-year-olds fared much better. However, in both math and science, the 13-year-olds ranked at the bottom, only ahead of students from Ireland, Portugal, and Jordan in science, and Portugal and Jordan in mathematics (fig. 1.4).

School curriculum appears to make the greatest difference in overall student performance. The top performing countries offer more demanding courses for 13-year-olds. In math, the greatest difference was the level of emphasis given to teaching algebra and geometry to 13-year-olds.

Science

Interest

Although children enter kindergarten with a wonderful curiosity about the natural world, it appears to be squelched for many children, particularly girls, within the early years of school. One reason that girls lose interest is that they are never exposed to the kind of information and experiences (working with tools, toys such as erector sets, etc.) needed to do well. It is generally believed that most of the scoring gap between boys and girls on science tests is the result of differential course taking, but this is only part of the answer. Researchers have also found a number of other reasons for the differences (Adelman, 1991; American Association of University Women, 1991; Daniels, 1990a; Oakes, 1990).

Several studies show conclusively that one reason for the scoring gap is that teachers at every level, of all ages and both sexes, discriminate in the classroom. The discrimination is both unintentional and unrecognized by teachers, except after they have seen themselves teaching via videotape

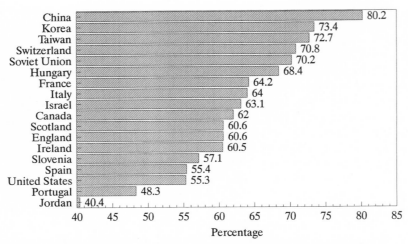

Figure 1.4. International math test, given at age 13: percentage correct, 1991.

Source: ETS. Graph by CPST.

(Eccles and Jacobs, 1986). There is also anecdotal evidence of discrimination against minority boys.

But teachers are not alone. Parents also discriminate against their daughters in failing to equip them with the most elementary training in the use of tools to build or repair mechanical things. The majority of American parents accept the myth that, solely because of their sex, their daughters are less talented mechanically and mathematically than their sons.[6] It also is apparent that girls who have not been exposed to mechanical tools and toys prior to junior high school are unlikely to learn later to "fix something" mechanical (Mullis and Jenkins, 1988).

Minority students, as a group, are more likely to be poor, to live in one-parent homes, and to attend inner-city schools with the smallest per capita science budgets. They are less likely, therefore, to have scientist role models of their own race or ethnicity, and they may be less likely to find science enrichment in their homes.

Another reason that children lose interest in science during the elementary years is that their teachers have taken few science courses. Although 88 percent had a college course in "methods of teaching science," only 72 percent had a course in any physical science, and only 44 percent had studied earth or space science (Weiss, 1989). Even those who took such courses report little or no college course work in science or mathematics in the past ten years.

It is no wonder, then, that many feel inadequate in teaching science, particularly the physical sciences and earth science. Only 27 percent of elementary teachers feel well qualified to teach life science; 15 percent feel qualified to teach physical or earth science (Weiss, 1989). The inadequate preparation in science of most K–8 teachers leads them to fear teaching science and to lack confidence in using hands-on activities in the classroom. Other research discussed below has demonstrated that hands-on participation is essential to maintaining student interest and understanding.

Women make up 94 percent of the teachers in K–3 classrooms, and 76 percent of those in grades 4–6 (Weiss, 1989). While their enthusiasm or fear of science will be transmitted to all the students, their attitudes have a particular effect on the girls in their classes. Nearly three out of four elementary school girls and over half of high school girls want to be teachers. Few adolescent boys, at any grade, aspire to a teaching career (American Association of University Women, 1991).

An additional factor, paramount in developing student attitudes toward science in elementary school, is opportunities for hands-on experimentation. Studies have shown the vital role played by such active participation, but many of today's classroom teachers have essentially no budget for even the simplest, least expensive materials or equipment. The National Science Teachers Association reports the average elementary school has $300 per year to spend on supplies and equipment (Aldridge, 1990). It is no surprise, then, that the typical elementary school teacher is limited to teaching the subject by assigning reading about science.

Coursework

Most students take a year of general science or earth science in the middle school years, and 95 percent of high school graduates have taken biology (Blank and Gruebel, 1993), generally in ninth grade. A recent study by the National Research Council (Committee on High School Biology Education, 1990) says that the teaching of biology is so unsatisfactory that "nothing short of a massive attack" involving major financial commitments could counter it. The panel found serious deficiencies in every aspect of the teaching of biology in elementary and secondary schools, and said that current instruction seems "designed to snuff out interest" in science, "failing to relate the science of life to the experience of living." The poor experience that high school students have with biology, which most of them take, discourages further interest in science. It is therefore no surprise that only 49 percent take chemistry, and less than half that number (21 percent) study physics (Blank and Gruebel, 1993). About half of all high school seniors have taken neither physics nor chemistry, and four-fifths have had no physics!

Another reason why students drop out of science as soon as possible is that they also have dropped out of mathematics. About 28 percent of all high school seniors are enrolled in a college-preparatory curriculum and score above average on tests of mathematics achievement, according to the American Institute of Physics (Czujko and Bernstein, 1989). Students with higher math achievement scores tend to take chemistry. There is no sex difference in this choice, given the math achievement level. Physics, however, is different. Regardless of mathematical excellence, girls are much less likely than boys to take physics. Some factor other than mathematical excellence is obviously at work.

Achievement

Unlike mathematics, for which girls score as well as boys in the elementary years, the NAEP science assessment shows a sex gap even at age 9 (Mullis et al., 1993). The gap has persisted, and sometimes widened, through each assessment from 1970 through 1990. By age 17, girls as a group are far behind boys in science.

The wide disparity between scores of minorities and nonminorities is slowly decreasing (see fig. 1.5). Scores of African American and Hispanic children age 9 and 13 improved substantially from 1977 to 1990, while scores of white students stayed essentially level. But the gap remains very large.

Problems in understanding elementary science are not limited to the girls and minority boys. Less than half of all American 17-year-olds selected the correct multiple choice answer to a simple question about measuring the volume of a block, even when provided with a picture to show how it was done. Only 3.4 percent of American 9-year-olds, 9.4 percent of 13-year-olds, and 41.4 percent of 17-year-olds chose the correct answer to the question (Mullis and Jenkins, 1988).

The relatively few U.S. students who take physics and chemistry lag behind the average students of other countries in these subjects as well as in mathematics. Most American students have taken biology by twelfth grade, but their test scores also are well below those of students in other nations in this field (Lapointe, Mead, and Phillips, 1989). Among thirteen countries, Americans rank thirteenth in biology, eleventh in chemistry, and ninth in physics.[7]

Like the international mathematics achievement tests, the earlier scores for this test are not reported by sex. However, the later 1988 and 1991 comparisons of science scores of 13-year-olds do provide the scores by sex (National Science Board, 1989; Mullis et al., 1993). Even by age 13, there is a significant gender gap in science achievement. It is larger in South Korea, Spain, Ireland, and the United States, and smaller in Taiwan, England, and Canada.[8]

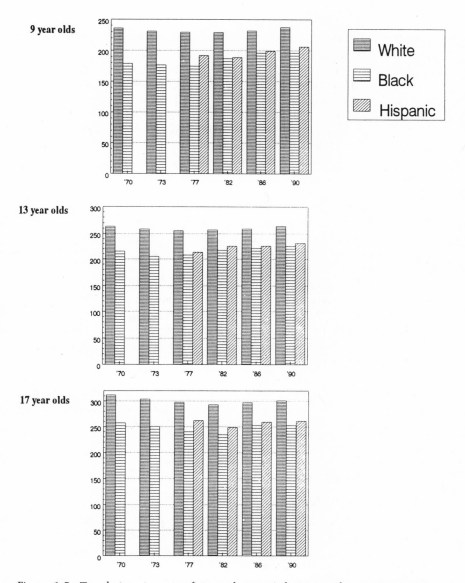

Figure 1.5. Trends in science proficiency by race/ethnicity and age, 1970–1990. Data not available for Hispanics for 1970 and 1973.

Source: NEAP/ETS. Graph by CPST.

High School Graduation

Only 7 out of every 10 American students currently graduate from high school. Factors that affect rates of high school graduation include geographic location, the social and economic status of students' families, ethnic background, and sex. Hispanics, our fastest growing minority population, are far less likely to finish high school than are either whites or African Americans. Asian Americans are more likely than whites to graduate from high school, and girls of every racial or ethnic group are more likely to finish than boys (Vetter, 1994).

Nationwide, the number of graduates declined from 1977 to 1993, when the number leveled off. Primarily because of population shifts, some states will have increasing numbers of high school graduates in coming years and some will have fewer. Most of the states that are gaining population, principally in the south and west, have low high school graduation rates, compared with states that are losing population (Zuniga, 1991), including those in the north. States with high minority populations also have lower graduation rates.

For example, California, with a growing population, has an above-average high school dropout rate (14.2 percent, compared with the U.S. average of 11.2 percent in 1990), and a high proportion of Asian (7.8 percent) as well as Hispanic (34.4 percent) and African-American (8.6 percent) students (California Department of Education, 1992).[9] The president and the nation's governors have set as a major goal for the year 2000 that at least 90 percent of American youth will graduate from high school (FCCSET, 1992). Based on the findings summarized thus far, the goal should include having each graduate complete a high school curriculum that keeps open his or her options for further choice. We have a long way to go to reach either goal.

College Enrollments

General Enrollment Patterns

Demographic changes in the college-age population are affecting enrollments, but not on a one-for-one basis. Although the nation has experienced a substantial drop in the number of college-age Americans eligible to attend higher education institutions, most institutions have kept their enrollments up by recruiting returning students, foreign students, and part-time students. A majority of returning and part-time students are women, who now make up more than half of all undergraduates and almost half of all graduate students. But women are underrepresented in the natural science and engineering fields, even at the undergraduate level.

Minority students are about half as likely to be enrolled in college as white students. Thus, in every state, the percentage of college students who are minorities is well below the comparable percentage in elementary and secondary schools. Nationwide, about 32 percent of all precollege students and 20 percent of all college students are members of minority groups (Vetter, 1994). As among women, non-Asian minority students are generally underrepresented in science and engineering.

Undergraduates in Engineering

As noted earlier, American freshmen began to indicate a decreasing interest in majoring in engineering, beginning in 1983. Freshman enrollments in engineering followed that pattern, with the drop occurring not only among white males, but among female and minority students as well (Engineering Workforce Commission, 1994). For women, representation remained at about 15 percent for almost a decade, after climbing steadily through the 1970s. A slight upturn in 1990–93 to 17.3 percent of undergraduates appears to indicate a new trend in interest.

The reduced share of freshmen indicating interest in majoring in engineering has meant that a smaller fraction of a shrinking population has entered engineering each year since 1982.[10] Freshman enrollment increases for all minorities and for women in the fall classes of 1990–93 have not offset enrollment decreases for white males, so that the class size has dropped an additional 5.4 percent in four years.

Bachelor's Degrees

Engineering

The number of B.S. degrees awarded in engineering averages about 67 percent of the number of students enrolled as engineering freshmen four or five years earlier (Engineering Workforce Commission, 1993, 1994). By this measure, the retention rates for the minority students are far lower than for the class as a whole—about 36 percent for African Americans, 54 percent for Hispanics, and 41 percent for Native Americans in 1992.

The addition of more women and minorities into engineering has not made up for the drop in the college-age population, so that the total number of baccalaureate graduates dropped by 14,530 (18.5 percent) in the six years from 1986 to 1992 (Engineering Workforce Commission, 1993).

Natural Sciences

Given the decline in student interest in all of the natural science fields beginning in 1982, it comes as no surprise that the number of baccalaure-

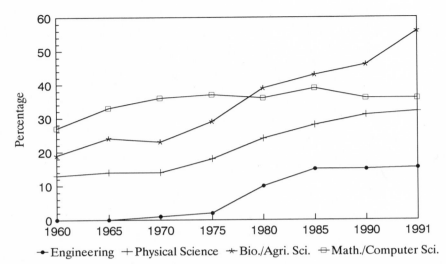

Figure 1.6. Percentage of women graduates with bachelor's in science and engineering, 1960–1991.

Source: NCES/NSF. Graph by CPST.

ate graduates in these fields began to drop four years later, despite the fact that the total number of baccalaureate degree awards continued to rise through 1991 (Vetter, 1994).

Following years of rapid growth in almost every field, women's participation in the natural sciences stabilized well below parity after 1965, then rose again in the eighties. However, by 1989, it was beginning to fall numerically and to level off in most fields as a percentage of the total (see fig. 1.6). Women's share of bachelor's degree awards in natural science and engineering fields has risen to 32 percent in 1991 (U.S. Department of Education, 1950–1991).

Non-Asian minorities earned almost 10 percent of all bachelor's degree awards in 1991 and 8 percent of those in natural science and engineering, compared with their 23 percent share of the college-age population. Asian American students earned 8 percent of the natural science and engineering baccalaureates, compared with their 4 percent share of all bachelor's degrees and of the college-age population (Vetter, 1994).

Graduate Education

At graduate levels, the momentum of earlier years is still reflected in increasing numbers and percentages of women earning master's and doctorate degrees, although the largest gain among new doctoral scientists and engineers has been in foreign graduates. Over the past decade, the number of doctoral degrees awarded in science and engineering has been stable at about 21,000 per year, rising to 25,250 by 1992. However, a significant and increasing fraction—38 percent in 1992—were earned by foreign citizens. Among 14,300 Americans earning doctorates in these fields each year, the total increasingly has included more women and fewer men. However, in the natural sciences (physical, mathematical, and life sciences) and in the engineering fields, only 9,428 doctorates were earned by U.S. citizens in 1992 and only 2,483 (26 percent) were earned by women (National Research Council, 1993b). A more detailed treatment of trends in science and engineering doctorate production is included in Chapter 6 below.

Women made up 25 percent of the full-time graduate enrollment in natural science and engineering fields in doctorate-granting institutions in fall 1991 (National Science Foundation, 1993). However, women are considerably more likely than men to stop with a master's degree. In most science fields, women now earn almost as high a percentage of master's degrees as they do of bachelor's degrees, but their share of the doctorates drops substantially (Vetter, 1994). They earn a much higher proportion of all degree awards than of those in all science and engineering fields, including the social and behavioral sciences. And they earn more of the degrees in all science and engineering fields than of those in the natural science and engineering fields, which exclude the social and behavioral group (fig. 1.7). But regardless of field, the percentage of bachelor's and master's degrees earned by women far exceeds the comparable percentage of doctorates.

In 1992, women earned only one-fourth of the U.S. doctorates in natural science and engineering, and more than one-half (52.8 percent) of those in the social and behavioral sciences (National Research Council, 1993b; National Science Foundation, 1993). Because women's percentage of graduate enrollments in natural science and engineering is no higher than their percentage of current Ph.D. awards in these fields, it appears that no substantial increase in women's share of these doctorates is likely to occur within the next several years.

The number of doctoral awards to American minorities continues to be so small that the prospect of increasing minority representation on college faculties remains dim.

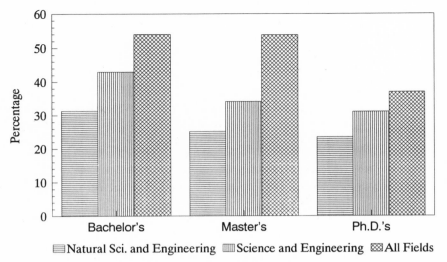

Figure 1.7. Percentage of women graduates, 1991. Data are for natural science and engineering fields, all science and engineering fields, and all fields.

Source: NCES/NSF. Graph by CPST.

Conclusion

The number of students graduating from high school is currently at its lowest level in a quarter century, and the proportion of those students who are qualified to elect science and engineering fields grows smaller each year as they progress through the precollege education system. Because of their sex or their race or ethnicity, some of the most capable students in our schools are being turned off to these fields.

As we move toward a new millennium, we find our children increasingly handicapped by poverty, drugs, single parent homes, and an education system that has not yet succeeded in preparing most of them to compete in an increasingly technological world. If this situation is to be improved, change must begin now, at both the precollege and college levels.

We do not know when our economy will require more professionals trained in science and engineering, but we do know that any serious attempt to increase the number of students eligible to choose college majors in science or engineering must take both sex and race/ethnicity into account. We can no longer afford to waste the talent in two-thirds of our increasingly diverse population.

Notes

1. Jaime Escalante, with his advanced placement calculus classes at Garfield High in East Los Angeles; Marva Collins and the children at Westside Prep in Chicago; the inner-city students at Franklin High in Philadelphia, who fence at near-Olympic level; and children at the Chad School in Newark who build and fly radio-controlled airplanes are a few examples.

2. Only 49 percent of the nation's eighth graders could answer the following question on the 1990 NAEP assessment: "The weight of an object on the Moon is $1/6$ of the weight of that object on the Earth. An object that weighs 30 pounds on Earth would weigh how many pounds on the Moon?"

3. The test was given to 26,000 students aged 11, 14, and 17 who attend public and private schools across the nation.

4. Even in kindergarten, minority children, except those who have participated in Head Start, score below majority children.

5. This study found that the teachers of the U.S. students who were tested were well trained and experienced. If they were atypical (although it is believed they were not), the findings are even more disturbing.

6. Conversely, most such parents also believe that their daughters are more talented verbally than their sons.

7. The U.S. students being tested were those in our college-preparatory track group, and they do not include students who have not taken these subjects.

8. It is notable that the U.S. students scored slightly higher than those of Ireland, French Ontario, and New Brunswick in 1988, but beat only Ireland, Portugal, and Jordan in 1991.

9. Although many of the Asian students, particularly among more recent immigrants, are completing high school at the head of their classes, and moving into the higher education system in large numbers, not all Asian American and immigrant Asian students perform well in school, and some students from all racial and ethnic groups drop out before finishing high school.

10. A slight increase in the size of the freshman class of fall 1988 and the graduating class of 1993 reflects the one-year increase in births in 1970.

CHAPTER 2

Investing in Human Potential: Policies and Programs in Higher Education

Marsha Lakes Matyas

In an ideal world, students of both sexes and all racial and ethnic groups would be encouraged to pursue career options in all fields, including science and engineering (S/E), and would be supported in their efforts. Ideally, there would be no sociocultural barriers that would discourage students or young professionals. Rather, children would have opportunities to explore a wide range of occupations and types of work and would have educational experiences that would keep a variety of career options open well into the undergraduate years. Unfortunately, current reality does not match this scenario. As detailed in Chapter 1, a variety of educational and social factors obstruct the pathway to a career in science and engineering for white male students and even more so for female and minority students.

Efforts to open up the pathway to S/E careers for underrepresented groups have typically taken the form of either institutional policies or intervention programs. Institutional policies are often designed to affect the particular aspects of campus academic or social life which influence women, minorities, and persons with physical disabilities in S/E studies. These include providing adequate financial aid for students, including aid for those with special needs due to a disability; monitoring student progress via routine calculation of attrition/retention and graduation rates by sex, racial and ethnic group, and disability status; providing S/E faculty role models from diverse racial and ethnic groups, of both sexes, and with a variety of physical disabilities; and actively working to create an overall campus climate that fosters success among female and minority students and those with physical disabilities.

Intervention programs usually consist of a series of activities that are organized for a group of targeted participants to address one or more specific factors or barriers affecting females' or minorities' interest, motivation, or skills in science, mathematics, or engineering. For example, a one-day career fair is organized to bring middle school children in contact with female and minority S/E role models so that they can (1) experience hands-on science activities; (2) learn about careers in S/E; (3) encounter positive role models of the same sex or racial and ethnic group; and (4) learn what steps they should take during middle and high school to pursue a career in science or engineering. Science, mathematics, and engineering intervention programs targeted at women and minorities have been active since the 1960s at both the precollege and the undergraduate levels. Science or engineering intervention programs targeted at persons with physical disabilities are rare.

Overview of Precollege Programs

In 1983, the American Association for the Advancement of Science (AAAS) Office of Opportunities in Science conducted an assessment of precollege programs that facilitated increased access and achievement of females, minorities, and students with physical disabilities in K–12 mathematics and science education (Malcom, 1984). Over 300 programs were surveyed. Of the 168 programs for which data were received, colleges and universities housed half of the projects focusing on women and two-thirds of those focusing on minority students. Nearly half of the projects were targeted exclusively at senior high school students.

Most of the projects were at least partially supported by the host institution, but nearly all received external funding as well. For women's projects, the top three funding sources were industry, private foundations, and student fees collected for that specific program. For minority programs, industry, foundations, and the National Science Foundation (NSF) were the top three sources of funding.

A variety of program types were identified which addressed many of the factors described in Chapter 1. Long-term programs tended to focus on the development of higher-level cognitive skills related to problem solving, understanding, and applications. Mathematics, Engineering, Science Achievement (MESA) programs are one example, working with minority students throughout junior and senior high school. Short-term projects usually focused on providing career information or course information relevant to students, teachers, and parents. Career fair programs (e.g., Expanding Your Horizons) are good examples. These programs appeared to be most effective when other systems designed to support the students' information and educational needs were present in the community.

Overview of Undergraduate and Graduate Efforts

Unfortunately, no study of undergraduate and graduate programs analogous to the AAAS precollege study has been undertaken. The best collection of information on minority programs at the undergraduate level is provided for programs in colleges and schools of engineering by the National Action Council for Minorities in Engineering (NACME).[1]

Minority engineering programs addressed both academic and attitudinal barriers that prevent minority students from earning engineering degrees. Specifically, the NACME study determined that model minority engineering programs contain the following components: (1) recruitment of students from high schools and two-year colleges; (2) monitoring of and assistance in admissions procedures; (3) assistance in student matriculation, including financial aid acquisition and budgeting, housing, diagnostic testing, academic advising, registration, and orientation; (4) academic support, including tutoring, study skills training, shadow courses or extra recitations, and course selection assistance; (5) student study centers; (6) linkages with student organizations, such as the National Society of Black Engineers, the Society for Hispanic Professional Engineers, and the Native American Science and Engineering Society; and (7) involvement in summer engineering jobs.

A comprehensive study of undergraduate programs for women in science has not been conducted. Until recently, there was no national organization coordinating programs targeted at women in science or engineering. In 1990, however, the directors of programs for women in engineering at Purdue University, Stevens Institute of Technology, and the University of Washington established the Women in Engineering Program Advocates Network (WEPAN). The goal of WEPAN is to facilitate recruitment, admission, retention, and graduation of women engineering students. Network activities focus on assisting and encouraging engineering schools throughout the United States to establish innovative programs for women in engineering or to expand the scope of existing programs.

According to a 1987 survey of prospective WEPAN members, the number and types of program activities for women in engineering has significantly declined over the last decade (Daniels, 1990b). With the exception of freshman scholarships and graduate fellowships, all types of program activities focusing on the recruitment and retention of women into engineering declined nationally between 1982 and 1987. These activities included student chapters of the Society of Women Engineers, availability of recruitment brochures and information targeted at women, programs for teachers and counselors, career conferences, summer programs, and junior high school outreach activities. This decline in activities focusing on women in engineering corresponds to the decline in the number of female freshman engineering students nationally, which also began in 1982 (American Association of Engineering Societies, 1989). Thus, while the national need for scientists and engineers is increasing, the number of women enrolling in engineering studies is decreasing and the efforts to recruit and retain them are becoming more sparse.

The Investing in Human Potential Study

Until recently, research on undergraduate and graduate programs for minorities and women in S/E consisted of isolated studies and fragmented data that failed to produce a comprehensive view of either the retention experience of the target groups or the extent and effectiveness of programs meant to increase their participation and retention in these fields. A more comprehensive study was needed to compile and analyze information describing current efforts by higher education institutions to recruit and retain women and minorities in these fields. To fill this need, the Investing in Human Potential (IHP) study was conducted. The study examined higher education institutions that were actively recruiting and retaining women, minorities, and persons with physical disabilities in S/E, as well as institutional policies and programs targeted at increasing the flow of talent into S/E. (For details on methodology, see Matyas and Malcom, 1991.)

The IHP study was conducted in four phases. In phase 1, institutions were selected for study. A decision was made to try to oversample institutions that were likely to have made specific efforts to encourage the participation of female and minority students and those with physical disabilities in science or engineering. Overall, 503 institutions were surveyed and 276 (55 percent) responded. Most of the responding institutions were research universities (61 percent), comprehensive colleges and universities (36 percent), or doctorate-granting institutions (16 percent; institution types refer to Carnegie classifications). A small number of liberal arts colleges also responded.

The study's first survey was designed to collect information from the president or chancellor about the institution as a whole and about how it approached recruitment, retention, and monitoring student progress (phase 2). Directors of specific programs and services at each institution received a follow-up survey designed to uncover information about the goals, history, and structure of the program; the target group of participants by sex, racial and ethnic group, educational level, and field of study; the program's impact via reported evaluation, publication, and dissemination; and the program's funding, staffing, and place within the institutional structure (phase 3).[2] The final phase of the study provided an opportunity to take a closer look at how programs, services, and policies at institutions combine to create an atmosphere that encourages the participation and achievement of the target group of students and faculty in science and engineering. Ten model institutions (each one a major research university, a women's college, or a minority institution) were chosen for intensive case studies. Only those institutions that had outstanding programs and services for at least two of the three target groups were chosen for a case study, and the sample of case study institutions was selected to include a variety of program models and geographic locations. Results of the IHP case studies are reported elsewhere (Matyas and Malcom, 1991); the results of phases 2 and 3 of the study are discussed in this chapter.

Institutional Factors

A number of institutional factors influence the learning environment and overall educational experience for students in higher education, thereby influencing the likelihood that a student will complete his or her degree. Some of these factors, such as "campus climate," financial aid, and faculty diversity are particularly critical for underrepresented students in S/E fields. The IHP study looked at some of these institutional factors.

The term "campus climate" has been used frequently in discussions of female and minority retention, especially for students in science or engineering majors. Shavlik, Touchton, and Pearson (1987, p. 7) describe campus climate for women as

> those aspects of the institutional atmosphere and environment which foster or impede women's personal, academic, and professional development. Campus climate issues include a wide range of individual behaviors and attitudes as well as institution-wide policies and practices, formal and informal, which reflect differential treatment of [students]. . . . With respect to students, climate issues include classroom and out-of-classroom experiences that affect the learning process. Regarding faculty and administrators, climate issues center on their professional experiences, characterized by subtle social and professional barriers which communicate to women that they are not quite first-class citizens in the academic community.

Integrating students into their institution's academic and social environment is clearly related to their persistence to graduation (Clewell and Ficklen, 1986). Though campus climate has many dimensions, the IHP study gathered information on two: general campus climate issues for women and minorities and institutional information-gathering activities. Nearly 90 percent of the institutions responding to the survey provided information about an institutional sexual harassment policy. Some, especially research universities and doctorate-granting institutions, also had conducted studies of campus climate issues for women and/or minorities.

Financial aid is another key factor in student enrollment and persistence in S/E studies. Stampen and Fenske (1988) reviewed the impact of financial aid on the participation of ethnic minorities in higher education, paying special attention to the plummeting minority enrollments in the late 1970s and the 1980s. They found that a number of factors inhibited the participation of African Americans, Hispanics, and Native Americans in higher education in the 1980s: rises in college costs; continuing inflation, which robs financial aid of its purchasing power; shift in aid from grants to loans; and higher admissions standards, especially in mathematics. All of these factors combine to make financial aid and tuition costs an important consideration, especially for underrepresented students. Previous studies also found that S/E students were more likely to receive financial aid of all kinds than were other students, even accounting for high grades, which qualify students for merit awards (U.S. Congress, 1989b). At the institutions in the IHP study, however, S/E students (59 percent) were no more likely to receive financial aid than were students in all majors (62 percent). This contrasting finding is probably due to the oversampling of historically black colleges and universities (HBCUs) and other traditionally minority institutions, at which a high percentage of students receive financial aid.

Minority and female faculty members are instrumental in recruiting and retaining all students, but especially female and minority S/E students. Specifically, they assist students by demonstrating competence in subject matter, including excellence in teaching, knowledge of subject matter, and sincere interest in students as individuals; mentoring, that is, "using one's own experiences and expertise to help guide the development of others"; and "intrusive advising," through frequent student contact to check on student academic progress and provide academic support as needed (Blackwell, 1988).

These types of activities can strongly influence female and minority students and those with physical disabilities to persist in science or engineering. However, minority and female faculty members must be established in secure and productive positions at the institution in order to influence student outcomes. Since the institutions in the IHP study were selected because of some demonstrated equity efforts, it was predicted that they would, collectively, have a significant resource pool of target group faculty members. This did not prove to be the case at most of the institutions responding.

In general, women still were found in the highest proportions in the non–tenure track positions in S/E. This is particularly detrimental because these positions are less likely to allow researchers to apply for independent grants, set up an independent program of research, or establish a long-term commitment to a teaching program at the institution. Similarly, relatively few S/E faculty members were minorities. This was especially true of the research universities and doctorate-granting institutions and least true at the comprehensive colleges and universities, which include many of the HBCUs.

On average, only 2.5 percent of total full-time non-HBCU faculty were African American. Like women faculty, the highest proportions of African American S/E faculty were found in non–tenure-track positions. These figures are similar to those found nationally where, in 1987, African Americans comprised only 2 percent of all S/E faculty, 1 percent of all full professors in S/E, and 2 percent of both associate professors and assistant professors in S/E (NSF, 1990d). Percentages for Hispanic faculty also were similar to national averages. The proportion of Native American faculty members was almost negligible. This finding was consistent among all institutional types and all S/E faculty types. There was a consistent and nearly complete absence of Native American faculty members in S/E at U.S. higher education institutions. Despite the fact that female and minority S/E faculty can play a vital role in expanding the flow of talent into S/E, their numbers on campus are small.

For all institutions, retention and its converse, attrition, are important concerns. For female and minority students in S/E, attrition rates are disproportionately high (U.S. Congress, 1989b; LeBold, 1987). Because data are not regularly collected for students with physical disabilities, their retention rates in S/E are largely unknown, although isolated studies indicate that attrition is as much as one-third higher for students with hearing impairments (Scherer in Jones and Watson, 1990).

In their 1986 study of effective institutional practices, Clewell and Ficklen found that systematic collection of data, monitoring, and follow-up are characteristics of institutions with successful retention of minority students. In the IHP study, this systematic monitoring process proved to be the exception rather than the rule: only 57 percent of colleges and universities responding to the survey routinely calculated attrition and graduation rates for undergraduate students. Furthermore, they were far more likely to calculate graduation and attrition rates routinely for undergraduate students than for graduate students (12 percent), and by racial and ethnic group (33 percent) than by sex (26 percent). Research universities were most likely to calculate both graduation and attrition rates by sex (44 percent) and by racial and ethnic group (59 percent) among all the institutional types.

Not only did few institutions routinely gather this information, but many were unable to gather it upon request. When asked to provide recent graduation and attrition rates by sex and by racial and ethnic group, many respondents noted that their databases would not allow them to calculate this information. More than a dozen institutional representatives called to ask the project staff for information on how they could calculate attrition rates and what the term "attrition" meant. Attrition rates for graduate students in S/E were especially difficult to obtain.

In summary, for many institutions there remains considerable work to be done, especially in the areas of S/E. Studies of campus climate and accessibility can help administrators identify specific problems in need of attention. A similar approach—exploratory research, identification of problems, implementation of action, and evaluation of results—needs to be applied specifically to issues of climate, faculty diversity, and student progress in S/E schools and departments.

Program Efforts for Women and Minorities

Information on 336 separate programs was collected by the phase 3 survey. The programs differed in their goals, the specific populations they targeted, their staffing and funding patterns, the extent to which they had been evaluated, and their particular niche in the institutional structure.

Program Types

Most of the programs responding to the survey primarily targeted students at the undergraduate level (57 percent). The largest group of programs focused on undergraduates in science and engineering (34 percent), followed by general undergraduate programs (23 percent), precollege (K–12) programs (20 percent), graduate programs (10 percent), and faculty programs (6 percent). Within these general categories, each program was classified by specific type.

Over one-third of the responding programs were undergraduate programs which specifically focused on the fields of science and engineering. There were a number of program types: (1) engineering recruitment and retention programs, which were the most common type of program ($N = 40$); (2) S/E recruitment and retention programs focusing on recruiting students in a variety of fields, which were also common ($N = 21$); and (3) national programs sponsored by the National Institutes of Health (NIH), which provided support for undergraduate and graduate minority students and faculty to conduct biomedical research at institutions with substantial minority student enrollment. These programs include Minority Access to Research Careers (MARC) ($N = 12$) and Minorities in Biomedical Research Studies (MBRS) ($N = 9$).

Other programs included: (1) scholarships for students in science and engineering fields ($N=9$); (2) bridge programs, which assisted students in the transition from high school to college, usually during the summer months ($N=8$); (3) campus chapters of professional associations, such as the Society of Women Engineers and the National Society of Black Engineers ($N=7$); (4) programs that introduced undergraduate students to research experiences but were not part of a national program such as MARC or MBRS ($N=4$); (5) science/mathematics learning centers, where students could seek assistance specifically in science and mathematics subjects ($N=3$); (6) president's or chancellor's task force on recruiting underrepresented groups into S/E and institutional studies on access to S/E by underrepresented groups ($N=2$); and (7) a re-entry program, where students had an opportunity to return to studies in S/E or to switch fields into S/E after being in the work force for a period of time ($N=1$).

Among the general undergraduate programs, there were seven specific types: (1) general retention programs, which provided academic support and counseling, usually for underserved or at-risk students ($N=21$); (2) general recruitment and admissions programs, which typically had special services for minority or at-risk students ($N=20$); (3) office of minority affairs, which focused on various issues, policies, and activities that affect minority students and staff on campus ($N=15$); (4) tutoring and study skills courses or centers, where students learned study skills or received tutoring in specific subjects ($N=9$); (5) office of women's affairs, which focused on various issues, policies, and activities that affect women on campus ($N=6$); (6) cultural centers, such as an African American cultural center that coordinated activities related to specific cultural groups ($N=4$); and (7) women's studies programs, which supported various activities and courses focusing on women ($N=2$).

Precollege programs (grades K–12) generally were one of five types: (1) high school science and engineering programs, including after-school and Saturday academy programs ($N=24$); (2) summer programs in science and engineering, typically residential programs in which students spent one to several weeks on campus ($N=18$); (3) career fairs and outreach recruiting programs, in which institutional personnel traveled to schools or brought students to campus to provide information on future career opportunities ($N=16$); (4) high school research apprenticeship programs, where students had opportunities to engage in research projects with assistance from scientists and engineers on campus ($N=9$); and (5) teacher in-service programs, where K–12 teachers upgraded their content and methods skills ($N=1$).

At the graduate level there were far fewer programs than at the undergraduate level. These programs were also divided into general and S/E categories. The general group includes ten general graduate recruitment and admissions programs, not specifically focusing on science or engineering. Among the graduate programs focusing on science or engineering, there were five major categories: (1) fellowships for research ($N = 10$); (2) health careers opportunities programs (HCOP), which provide scholarships for students in training for health professions ($N = 5$); (3) graduate recruitment and retention programs in science or engineering ($N = 4$); (4) seminars for graduate students who will work as teaching assistants ($N = 2$); and (5) bridge programs, which assist students in the transition from undergraduate studies to graduate studies, typically during the summer months ($N = 2$).

Some institutions reported having specific programs to recruit or retain faculty members from underrepresented groups. Generally, these efforts fell into one of three categories: (1) S/E faculty recruitment effort ($N = 15$); (2) affirmative action office or office of professional development ($N = 5$); and (3) faculty women/minority faculty associations ($N = 1$).

Target Population

In addition to the educational level of the participants, programs were classified according to the primary target population for the program. Over half of all the programs responding to the survey were targeted at minority students or faculty (table 2.1), including programs that were targeted specifically at minority group members or at "all students, with special efforts for minorities." This was true for programs at the precollege, undergraduate, and graduate levels. Programs targeted at both women and minorities accounted for an additional 28 percent of the responding programs. Very few programs were targeted exclusively at women (or at "all students with special efforts for women"). At the graduate level, only one program was targeted at women.

The survey also asked whether the program included activities for parents of students. As the educational level of the program increased, the likelihood that parents were involved decreased. Parents play a key role in the development of students' interest and persistence in S/E fields. Approximately 52 percent of precollege programs and 49 percent of general undergraduate programs included parent components. Significantly fewer undergraduate S/E programs did so (30 percent), and parent components were rare at the graduate level.

Participants

The number and type of participants involved in each program varied according to the specific program type. In total, 144,739 participants were involved in the 336 programs responding to the survey. White participants (46 percent) and African American participants (29 percent) accounted for three-quarters of all program participants. Hispanics accounted for an additional 15 percent and Native Americans accounted for 3 percent. The pro-

Table 2.1. Target Groups for Intervention Programs, by Program Type

	Percentage (Number) of Programs for Target Groups*			
Program Type	Minorities	Women	Women and Minorities	Other
Precollege (K–12)	50 (34)	12 (8)	35 (24)	3 (2)
Undergraduate, general	50 (38)	5 (4)	22 (17)	22 (17)
Undergraduate, S/E†	58 (38)	10 (12)	25 (29)	7 (8)
Graduate, general	50 (5)	0	50 (5)	0
Graduate, S/E†	52 (12)	4 (1)	26 (6)	17 (4)
Faculty	25 (5)	20 (4)	35 (7)	20 (4)
Total	51 (160)	9 (29)	28 (88)	11 (35)

*Minorities includes programs targeted at "minorities only" and "all students with special efforts for minorities." Women includes programs targeted at "women only" and "all students with special efforts for women." Women and Minorities includes programs targeted at "women and minorities only" and "all students with special efforts for women and minorities" (Matyas and Malcom, 1991, p. 92).
†Science and engineering.

portion of African American program participants was consistently high among all of the program types, with the exception of faculty programs, where white participants were most prevalent.

Participant data were also examined to determine whether programs targeted at women serve minority students (i.e., minority women) and whether programs targeted at minority students serve women. Programs targeted at women had especially low average percentages of African American (7 percent) and Hispanic (8 percent) participants, and those targeted at "women and minorities" had lower average percentages of African American (40 percent) and Hispanic (14 percent) participants than did programs targeted at minorities only or "all students with special efforts for minorities" (58 percent for African Americans and 19 percent for Hispanics). A similar pattern occurred for Native Americans, while the pattern was reversed for whites. Programs for women had high percentages of white participants (70 percent, on average) and programs for minorities had low percentages of white participants (8 percent). In short, programs targeted at "minorities only" or "all students with special efforts for minorities" had the highest percentages of minority participants, while those for "women only" or "all students with special efforts for women" involved low percentages of minorities. Therefore, programs targeted at women do not appear to serve minority women very well.

Do programs targeted at minority students serve women? Results indicate that they do, but with room for improvement, especially among certain minority groups. About 51 percent of the participants in programs targeted at minorities are female. However, this varies among the racial and ethnic groups. Women comprise only 38 percent of the Native Americans, 38 percent of the Puerto Ricans, 43 percent of the Mexican Americans, and 44 percent of the other Hispanics involved in programs targeted at minorities. Women in these four racial/ethnic groups were also underrepresented in programs targeted at "women and minorities." Therefore, programs for minorities and for women and minorities seem to do a good job of recruiting African American women into their activities but are not as successful with Hispanics and Native Americans.

Amount and frequency of contact with program participants varied by program type. Precollege and undergraduate program (both general and S/E) staffs were most likely to have frequent contact with participants. In fact, 64 percent of precollege programs and 59 percent of undergraduate S/E programs involved students in program activities at least once weekly. Graduate and faculty level programs were most likely to meet on an "as needed" basis. Interestingly, the frequency of contact with participants also differed by target group. Programs targeted at women were much less likely to meet with participants at least once per week (33 percent) than were programs targeted at minorities (59 percent) or women and minorities (54 percent). Thus, participants involved in programs at the graduate and faculty levels, or in programs targeted at women, had a less time-intensive intervention experience.

Staffing and Funding

In Malcom's (1984) study of effective precollege programs, she found that one of the key factors in successful programs was the program staff: their commitment and their effectiveness. In this study, the staff of the programs also reflected the target audience they served. Programs targeted at minorities had high percentages of minority employees and moderate proportions of female employees. Programs targeted at women had low percentages of minority employees and high percentages of white female employees. The job descriptions for program employees were not described in detail. However, staff in effective intervention programs function as role models for participants, often just by being successful, professional employees at a college or university. Therefore, the presence of target group-appropriate staff members may play a key role in the success of these programs.

In addition to paid staff, many programs utilize student (40 percent) and faculty (56 percent) volunteers. Use of volunteers differed somewhat by program type. General undergraduate programs were most likely to use student volunteers (59 percent), probably as tutors. Faculty programs were most likely to involve faculty volunteers (73 percent), but around half of all other program types used faculty volunteers as well. Programs targeted at women were especially likely to utilize faculty and student volunteers, compared to programs for minorities or women and minorities.

The most recent sources of funding for each program also were examined. Respondents described the percentage of funding received from the host institution, federal government, state government, business and industry, private foundations, and other sources for the most recent year. Over half of the programs depended upon a single source of funds, and an additional 34 percent depended on only two sources of funding. Less than 15 percent of the programs had a funding base of three or more sources. This was consistent among the program types and the programs targeted at women versus minorities. Faculty programs (65 percent) and general undergraduate (61 percent) and graduate (49 percent) programs received the highest proportions of funding from the host institution, while undergraduate and graduate S/E programs received the highest proportions of federal funds. Precollege programs, as a whole, had the most balanced funding profile, with significant amounts of funding coming from the host institution, federal and state grants, and donations from business and industry. Precollege, undergraduate, and graduate S/E programs are, therefore, not as likely to be mainstreamed into departmental or institutional budgets as to be externally funded by grants for program efforts or research grants that include support for graduate students.

Further data partially confirmed this hypothesis. Most of the programs (56 percent) functioned as a set of discrete activities, and components of the program have not been mainstreamed or institutionalized into the activities of the host institution. However, programs specifically focused on science or engineering were least likely to have mainstreamed activities at the precollege (31 percent had mainstreamed at least one component), undergraduate (46 percent) or faculty levels (33 percent). Also, programs targeted at women (32 percent) were less likely than those targeted at minorities (47 percent) or women and minorities (52 percent) to have mainstreamed program components.

Some programs (16 percent) also generated support by charging participant fees. Programs targeted at women were significantly more likely to charge fees than were programs targeted at minorities or at women and minorities.

Evaluation

As noted earlier, most intervention programs have not been evaluated extensively; programs in the IHP study are not an exception. Only 40 and 50 percent of precollege and undergraduate programs, respectively, had completed a formal report or longitudinal analysis of their program's effectiveness, depending upon specific program type. Graduate programs were just as likely to have conducted an informal tally of the students served by the program as to have conducted a more formal evaluation of the program (23 percent each). A large proportion of the programs (38 percent) indicated that they had undertaken some type of evaluation but did not provide any further information. This was especially true for general graduate recruitment programs (67 percent) and for undergraduate S/E programs (48 percent).

Respondents also were asked to detail which components of their program seemed to be most effective and which were least effective in accomplishing the program's goals. The most effective components and strategies are listed here in the approximate order of their frequency: (1) overnight, residential, or summer programs;[3] (2) one-on-one interaction with faculty members;[4] (3) hands-on laboratory experience;[5] (4) active recruitment and identification of potential program participants; (5) tutoring and counseling services provided by the program, as noted by general undergraduate programs; (6) academic course work done in conjunction with the program; (7) study groups, support groups, and student mentors; (8) financial support for participants, especially for graduate S/E programs; (9) opportunities to meet or work with role models and to take field trips to S/E work sites; and (10) career conferences and outreach activities.

For the most problematic program components as identified by survey respondents, at least three programs identified the following: (1) career fairs and one-time outreach activities are not effective in recruiting female and minority students (most frequently noted by both undergraduate and graduate general recruiting programs); (2) lack of financial support for students and for the program creates difficulties in program operation and effectiveness (most commonly mentioned by undergraduate and graduate S/E programs); (3) recruiting students for the program is difficult (most often noted by undergraduate S/E programs); (4) tutoring is not effective (most often noted by undergraduate S/E programs); (5) using traditional classroom strategies such as lecture and discussion are not effective (especially noted by precollege programs); (6) providing a campus residential experience for participants is costly; (7) large requirements of time from faculty members makes it difficult for many faculty members to participate; (8) field trips, academic skills seminars, and social activities are not effective; and (9) lack of staff training is problematic.

Institutional Niche

Intervention programs in S/E often begin as a separate set of activities funded by external sources (such as a federal grant) and directed by a nonfaculty member. However, their long-term survival and effectiveness hinge upon the support and commitment of the host institution. The IHP survey asked specific questions about how the program functioned within the institution and about the support it received from various institutional administrators and faculty members.

Programs were housed in a variety of departments and offices. Precollege and undergraduate S/E programs were most likely to be housed within the school or department of engineering (20 percent and 41 percent, respectively). General recruitment and retention programs for undergraduates primarily were located in offices of student affairs (20 percent) and admissions offices (15 percent). Both general (71 percent) and science/engineering (45 percent) graduate programs were located in the graduate school. Programs for faculty members were dispersed among a variety of offices, but 25 percent were housed within the provost's office.

Program directors also rated the overall support that the program had received from top institutional administration (president/chancellor, vice-presidents, deans), administrators of departments and schools with whom they work, and faculty of departments and schools with whom they work. Each of these groups received high ratings for support; "excellent" ratings were given by large percentages of programs to top administration (56 percent), departmental administrators (48 percent), and faculty members (43 percent).

There were some differences in perceived support among the program types, however. Both undergraduate and graduate S/E program directors perceived that top administration was significantly more supportive than was the faculty. Similarly, directors of general undergraduate programs perceived that the program received more support from departmental administrators than from faculty members. Overall, program administrators felt that they were receiving excellent support, especially from the top administration of the institution.

In sum, a wide variety of intervention program types are in operation at higher education institutions. Many of these programs demonstrate characteristics typical of exemplary intervention efforts (Malcom, 1984; Landis, 1985; Clewell and Ficklen, 1986; Clewell, Anderson, and Thorpe, 1992). Few of the survey respondents reported efforts to disseminate their program models to other institutions, however. This lack of dissemination and the limited number and types of effective programs focused on women hampers the potential national impact of S/E intervention efforts.

Efforts for Students with Physical Disabilities

According to section 504 of the Rehabilitation Act of 1973, higher education institutions are "required to make reasonable adjustments and change discriminatory policies so that qualified students with disabilities can fulfill academic requirements. Students are not to be excluded from programs because of physical barriers or the absence of auxiliary aids" (ACE, 1989). The 504 regulations do not identify or describe a single acceptable method for offering these services to students with disabilities, however. Most institutions do so through an office for students with disabilities (OSD). Nearly three-fourths of the 276 institutions responding to the IHP survey had an OSD. Colleges and universities do not have S/E recruitment programs targeted at students with physical disabilities as they do for female and minority students. For students with disabilities, the OSD is the primary source of help. The IHP study examined how the needs of students with physical disabilities who are majoring in science or engineering are met by sending a special survey to OSDs at the participating institutions; 45 percent of those offices ($N = 92$) responded.

Support Services for Science-Related Studies

Students with physical disabilities must negotiate a variety of barriers to complete their undergraduate or graduate studies. Depending upon their particular disability, they may require one or more of the following forms of assistance: physical accommodations allowing them access to the campus, to specific buildings, and to specific classrooms (e.g., curb cuts and elevators); alternative methods for obtaining information provided during lectures and recitations (e.g., note-takers, assertive listening devices, and interpreters); adaptations in printed classroom materials (e.g., textbooks on audiocassette); and accommodations allowing them access to other campus services, such as placement centers and libraries.

For students with physical disabilities who major in S/E fields, some additional barriers may be encountered. First, although regular classrooms and lecture halls may be generally accessible to mobility-impaired students, the laboratory classrooms may be inaccessible because there are no elevators and door openings may be too small to accommodate a wheelchair. Further, most laboratory classrooms do not have benches built to accommodate students with some disabilities.

Second, the equipment used in laboratory work often must be adapted for use by students with disabilities. For example, students with hearing impairments may need instruments with visual readouts rather than instruments with auditory signals, while students with visual impairments may need instruments with auditory signals. A variety of modifications in laboratory equipment may be required for students whose mobility is impaired. The general rule in laboratory settings should be that, whenever possible, the student should do as much of the hands-on work as his or her disability will allow. "Watching" or "listening" while someone else performs the laboratory work does not have the same value as "doing." When a disability prevents the student from doing the laboratory work alone, a partner may be utilized. However, the student with the disability should continue to be actively involved in making decisions concerning methods, observing and recording results, manipulating raw data via calculation, and drawing conclusions.

A third consideration for students with physical disabilities is acquiring usable classroom notes and textbooks. Ideally, the note-taker should be someone familiar with the content area or at least be at the same level of study in the content area as the student with the physical disability. Often, a fellow student in the class is called upon to perform this service. Acquiring audiotaped or Braille textbooks for science, mathematics, or engineering courses is a greater challenge for two reasons. First, many texts in these fields become quickly outdated; every year there is a new "standard" text in the field. Second, recording these texts and translating equations, figures, and graphics into audio or Braille descriptions requires skills in both the specific content area and in the specific type of translation. Recently, Recording for the Blind, Inc., a national organization that provides requested books on audiocassette, recruited more than 600 scientists and engineers nationwide to volunteer to act as readers for texts in their fields.

The fourth barrier S/E students with physical disabilities often face is forging a working relationship with S/E faculty members and graduate teaching assistants. Since few students with physical disabilities major in science or engineering fields, most S/E faculty have had few, if any, students with disabilities in their classrooms. Consequently, faculty have had little or no experience or training in providing the support services needed by students with disabilities. In most cases, it becomes the student's responsibility to approach the faculty member, explain the nature of his or her disability, and suggest the adaptations needed for the course. This requires that the student already knows the course and laboratory content—a situation which is rarely the case.

Finally, science, mathematics, and engineering courses and research increasingly utilize personal and mainframe computers and specialized software. Appropriate hardware and software must be available so that students with various disabilities can access the keyboards and effectively utilize the software. For example, students with visual impairments may need additional software and hardware to convert information generated by course-specific software to synthetic speech output or refreshable Braille.

How do OSDs respond to the special needs of students with physical disabilities who major in science or engineering? The majority of students served by the OSDs in this study were nonscience majors (70 percent). Only 16 percent of all students served were S/E majors and only 14 percent of students with physical disabilities were in S/E majors. Therefore, OSD staff may have had fewer opportunities to develop working relationships with S/E faculty members compared to non–S/E faculty members. Also, since students with disabilities are rarely found in S/E departments, faculty members in those departments have limited opportunities to learn how to assess and fulfill the needs of these students.

The IHP survey presented each OSD with three hypothetical situations, describing the assistance which might be required by a student with a specific physical disability who is majoring in science or engineering. The OSDs provided details on how they would handle each of the following situations: a student with a hearing impairment in engineering who requested oral interpreters for large lecture courses; a student with a mobility impairment who requested a laboratory assistant for a chemistry course; and a student with a visual impairment who requested specific technology and services for a calculus course.

In all of the survey responses to these hypothetical situations, it was clear that most OSD staff would make every effort to provide the services needed by the student and to locate funding to pay for the services. However, in many cases a sense of helplessness and hopelessness was apparent. In some cases, this arose from a lack of adequate funds (both internal and external) to pay for all of the student services and equipment needed. In others, it was caused by a lack of trained personnel, such as interpreters, in the vicinity of the institution. In many cases, the respondents indicated that they simply could not provide all the services and equipment requested and had strong doubts that appropriate funds and equipment could be found. A number of respondents said it would be the student's responsibility to come up with at least part of the funds or equipment.

When faced with a diverse group of requests for student services and equipment, OSDs often have to find ways to optimize use of limited funds and personnel. For example, students may be encouraged to enroll in courses for which an interpreter has already been assigned for the coming semester or quarter. The student may find it easier to major in areas where a number of students with his or her type of disability are already enrolled, simply because it is easier to get access to interpreters, lecture notes, and other services or because the faculty in these fields are already familiar with the staff and services of the OSD. Ultimately, students who want to enroll in courses that are atypical for students with disabilities (such as S/E courses) may find that they must wait a semester or quarter until interpreters are available or until equipment is ready. With the sequential nature of many S/E curricula, this waiting game becomes not only frustrating but costly for the student. The efforts of the OSD to serve as many students as possible while utilizing limited staff and funds can unintentionally serve a "gatekeeper" function, steering students with physical disabilities away from nontraditional majors such as S/E (NSF, 1990b).

Recommendations

The results of the IHP study suggest policies and programs that may be useful to all institutions. The recommendations of the study are organized around three themes: institutional policies, programs for women and minorities, and programs for students with disabilities.

Institutional Policies

Institutions must renew their commitment to provide campus environments that foster full academic and social integration of diverse students and faculty. Campus climate is not static; progress and regression occur. As formal barriers to equity are removed, informal and more subtle barriers may continue to impede full participation of underrepresented or nontraditional groups of students and faculty, especially in S/E. Progress of students, especially female and minority students and those with physical disabilities, must be carefully monitored to determine where attrition is occurring; monitoring should be done at the departmental level. Cultivating a positive campus climate may require regular and increasingly fine-tuned studies, implementation of appropriate policies, especially concerning financial aid, and training of faculty and staff. Institutions that have not already done detailed studies of campus accessibility to persons with disabilities should do so. Institutions that have conducted general access studies should initiate collaborative studies between OSDs and S/E departments to examine access to S/E classrooms, laboratories, and equipment.

Finally, given the finding that very few institutions reported having programs targeted only on faculty recruitment or retention, more explicit effort is needed to increase the number of female and minority faculty and of those who either come to the institution with a physical disability or acquire one once there. Specific strategies for recruiting and retaining female and minority faculty members have been suggested (for details, see Blackwell, 1988, and Sposito, 1992) and should be utilized.

Programs for Women and Minorities

In order to maximize their impact, improvements and revisions in the structure and activities of S/E recruitment and retention programs are needed. First, these programs should not be isolated efforts on a campus. Rather, some coordination or, at minimum, regular communication should occur among programs. Programs specific to life sciences, chemistry, physics, and engineering share some common goals, common program activities, and common problems. By sharing strategies and coordinating some activities, separate programs might be able to function more cost-effectively and, consequently, to expand program activities and services. Ideally, these programs should function as stepping-stones to permanent structural reforms in the university climate; this evolution of intervention efforts is detailed further elsewhere (Matyas and Malcom, 1991).

Recruitment of participants—both students and faculty—is a key issue in program improvement. Many institutions reported having difficulty achieving this objective. In general, programs must expand their recruitment efforts into new areas. Precollege and undergraduate programs can establish relationships with churches, with parochial schools, and with such community-based organizations as youth clubs and Urban Leagues. Graduate and faculty programs can establish ongoing partnerships with administrators and S/E faculty at higher education institutions that serve large proportions of minority students to develop a pipeline of minority graduates interested in their programs. In the case of faculty members, institutions may need to develop relationships with potential faculty members early, during or prior to their entrance into graduate school.

In addition, recruitment efforts must be expanded to new areas. The study found imbalances in the distribution of program participants. In general, this distribution was limited by the results of initial recruitment efforts. In terms of the racial and ethnic identity of program participants, a special effort should be made to recruit male and female Native Americans and Hispanic females. These groups were rarely represented in the programs that responded to the IHP surveys. In addition, programs targeted toward women must make efforts to recruit more minority women into their programs. Increased participation of minority women among the staff of such programs may be a critical first step to increasing their proportions among program participants.

About half the precollege and undergraduate programs involved parents. Parents play a key role in student enrollment and retention. Parental involvement in efforts targeted toward students is critical, even at the undergraduate and graduate levels. Programs should make efforts to help parents understand how and why students become scientists and engineers (including the training required and job opportunities available), how the program activities can assist students in reaching their goals, and how parents can assist their children in this process. Similarly, the role of "significant others" should be examined, especially at the graduate and faculty levels. The financial and emotional support (or lack of support) from spouses and parents can make the difference in whether a graduate student persists through degree completion. Program and departmental activities should be established to help these key persons understand the graduate education and tenure processes.

Although they are costly and staff-intensive, residential campus experiences (overnight, summer, and bridge programs) are extremely effective and should be continued and expanded. By helping students become comfortable in the campus setting, they build confidence and skills necessary for the successful transition from secondary school to collegiate work. Conversely, the use of one-time outreach programs for generating interest in science and engineering should be carefully considered. In order to be effective, one-time outreach programs should include activities for parents and teachers as well as for students, have a specific focus on sparking interest among female and minority students, and be accompanied by follow-up activities for students (such as campus visits or personal letters and calls from current undergraduate students).

In terms of new programs, a rejuvenation of efforts to recruit and retain women in S/E is needed.[6] Some effective precollege and undergraduate program models and materials are available, but dissemination of these models must be funded and evaluated. Programs targeted at women need to be structured more like those for minority students, including multiyear involvement with students, strong academic components, increased contact with students (daily or weekly), and reduced-fee or no-fee programs. At the graduate and faculty levels, effective models are scarce. As they are developed, these program models should be based as much as possible on educational research findings, and should be implemented, extensively evaluated, revised, and broadly disseminated.

Finally, the study found little effort being made to evaluate thoroughly the effects of these programs. Evaluation must be an integral component of intervention programs, not an "add-on" at the program's completion. Specific program goals should be set and evaluation methods designed to assess those goals. Program staff should utilize evaluation consultants as needed to assist in the design, implementation, and analysis of the evaluation. The evaluation should not be "turned over" to an outside consultant; the program staff must be involved in each aspect of the evaluation in order to make it a productive effort that informs program design and operation.

Funding agencies and institutional administrators should require program directors to provide evidence that specific program goals have been set, a detailed plan of evaluation has been constructed, and a regular method for reporting evaluation results has been established. Funders also should provide program directors with training in how to develop and implement program evaluation and, subsequently, with the funds necessary to conduct a proper evaluation and the time necessary to measure results (preferably a number of years).

Efforts for Students with Physical Disabilities

The Americans with Disabilities Act (ADA) went into effect only very recently, in 1992. The implications of this act are tremendous for students with disabilities, yet the reality of their situation may look very different from what the ADA proposes. In 1973—before the ADA was passed—federal law already stated that "colleges, universities, and other postsecondary institutions are required to make reasonable adjustments and change discriminatory policies so that qualified students with disabilities can fulfill academic requirements. Students are not to be excluded from programs because of physical barriers or the absence of auxiliary aids" (ACE, 1989, p. 24). Nevertheless, in the IHP study, many institutions were unable to comply with the letter and spirit of the 1973 law in the types of services they were able to offer to the hypothetical S/E students the IHP survey described. With shrinking budgets, it is unlikely that these services will improve dramatically in the immediate future despite the requirements of the ADA and, therefore, unlikely that campus-wide services will be able to serve all student needs.

Departments of science and engineering as well as the staff of OSD offices will have to make a clear commitment to providing students with physical disabilities full access to training in these fields. This requires both the department in which the student is enrolled and the OSD to take an active role in assessing whether a lack of needed equipment, interpreters, or other services is acting as a gatekeeper, preventing the student from making normal progress toward his or her educational goals. Departments (or institutions within the same geographic area) may be able to generate a pool of adapted equipment available for loan or rental during semesters when it is needed.

With assistance from the OSD staff and the staffs of national organizations such as AAAS, S/E departments could assess laboratory facilities, course software and hardware, equipment, and classroom facilities specifically for accessibility and possible adaptation. With support from the NSF, the AAAS currently is working with engineering schools around the country to develop models for creating access to engineering education for students with disabilities.

Because the doors to a future career in S/E can be closed early in adolescence, S/E departments, OSDs, and other university departments should form coalitions with area community-based organizations to provide outreach activities to children in grades K–12 who have physical disabilities. Outreach activities should include parents of these children.

Finally, in order to provide role models for students with physical disabilities, specific efforts must be made to recruit and retain S/E faculty members who come to the institution with a physical disability or who acquire a physical disability while at the institution. These faculty are critical role models for students who rarely have the opportunity to know a person with a similar disability who is working in a science or engineering field.

Summary

Previous studies have shown that creating an atmosphere that promotes diversity among the S/E faculty and the student body requires focusing on both policies and programs and on both academic and social life on campus. The current study suggests that the approach an institution takes toward creating an atmosphere for diversity may differ by institutional type. Regardless of the specific strategies used, however, institutional commitment is the required first step: "High levels of institutional commitment tend to lead to the development of comprehensive strategies addressing a broad range of the causes and correlates of attrition" (Jones and Watson, 1990, p. 70). The key to improving the situation is to translate need into commitment and commitment into effective action.

Notes

1. In 1985, NACME commissioned the National Association of Minorities Engineering Program Administrators (NAMEPA) to document how support programs for underrepresented minority students within colleges and schools of engineering should be developed (Landis, 1985). Unfortunately, their study did not include science programs.

2. Contrasts were limited to programs that focused on increasing the participation of female or minority students and students with physical disabilities in S/E.

3. Undergraduate S/E programs were most likely to cite this component as critical in their success.

4. This was especially noted by precollege and undergraduate S/E programs.

5. Laboratory experience was mentioned most often as a critical component by precollege programs.

6. For an overview of current information on this issue, see also Matyas and Dix, 1992.

CHAPTER 3

Barriers to Women's Participation in Academic Science and Engineering

Henry Etzkowitz, Carol Kemelgor, Michael Neuschatz, and Brian Uzzi

For women there are, undoubtedly, great difficulties in the path, but so much the more to overcome," exulted Maria Mitchell (1818–89), the first female professor of astronomy at the then newly founded Vassar College. More than a century later, on the 175th anniversary of her birth, women's scientific aspirations are still restricted by "tradition and authority" (Enna, 1993). When attention is focused on issues of women in science in the 1990s, it is usually directed at undergraduate and K–12 education, with numerous programs targeted at these levels (Matyas, 1993).

Conflicting demands of career aspirations, personal responsibilities, and the requirements of a male-oriented academic structure place female Ph.D. students and junior faculty in a "triple bind." The traditional male-oriented organization and culture of the doctoral program creates a series of invisible (and visible) barriers to women that are difficult to overcome. These blockages are exacerbated by traditional female socialization and the desire of most women for a personal life beyond the work site. Even as taken for granted academic practices continue to work against them, most women in science do not want to be "men." Instead, many attempt to legitimize a female "relational" model of doing science (*Science*, 1992).

In this chapter we focus on the experiences of women in Ph.D. programs and as faculty members. Rather than examining threshold effects that might keep women out of graduate programs, or glass ceiling effects that might keep women with high quality training from progressing to the peak of academic careers, we investigated the conditions under which women are at a disadvantage during their doctoral training and early stages of their academic careers. Academic practices, presumed to be meritocratic and gender-free, often work against women's professional success. Their deleterious effects on most women are sometimes hidden behind a neutral or even positive facade erected on the highly publicized achievements of a few exceptional women, some of whom deny the existence of obstacles in their path (*Science*, 1992). We recognize that men have some of these same experiences as well as different ones. However, the lack of social and professional connections available to most women in academic science and engineering departments, in concert with overt and covert gender bias and differences in socialization, creates special and unique problems for women.

Data and Methods

The initial research site is classified as a Carnegie 1 research university (Boyer, 1987). To determine the receptivity of their cultures to women graduate students and faculty members, four departments were selected for examination: (1) physics, (2) chemistry, (3) electrical engineering, and (4) computer science.[1] In the 1987–88 academic year, 350 students and 76 dropouts were identified in the four departments, along with 198 students who had received their doctorates within the previous five years.

In these departments, there are 117 faculty members, including 5 women, two each in computer science and physics and one in chemistry. Women represent only 4.2 percent of the faculty members in these departments. At the time faculty data were collected, only one of the women was tenured. During the course of the study another was granted tenure; she was apparently the first woman accorded permanent status in the engineering school.[2]

We collected data from departmental academic records on advisors and advisees and we interviewed female and male faculty members, female graduate students, and academic administrators. The quantitative data consist of a listing of current graduate students, along with Ph.D. recipients over the last five years, paired with their main faculty advisors (from one of the departments, electrical engineering, data on Ph.D. recipients span only the previous two years). Supplementing this, data were also gathered for students who dropped out of their programs prior to earning their doctorate. In the computer science and physics departments, dropout information was obtained for the previous five years, while in chemistry it spans three years, and in electrical engineering only one.[3]

The qualitative data consists of forty-seven interviews with faculty, graduate students, and administrator informants. Twenty-five interviews were conducted with female Ph.D. students who were currently attending or had recently graduated from the physics, chemistry, electrical engineering, and computer science departments. Interviews were conducted with all five female faculty members. Two recent former women faculty members who are currently faculty members at other universities were also interviewed. Interviews were conducted with eight male faculty members who had been identified by chairs or graduate students as having either particularly good or poor relations with female graduate students. Chairs were also interviewed to ascertain whether there were any special departmental policies concerning the recruitment of women. (There were none.) Interviews were also conducted with administrators in the engineering and graduate schools: a dean, an assistant provost, and an affirmative action officer.

Women's experience as faculty members and graduate students was studied in the same four disciplines at a public research university. In addition, a department of molecular biology with a critical mass of women faculty was studied at a third university, bringing to a total of nine the number of departments we studied. In this chapter we primarily report on the qualitative findings from the initial site. We also draw upon findings from our current study of programs to improve the condition of women in science in graduate school (see Etzkowitz and Fox, 1991).

Caveats

We caution the reader to place the discussion of findings reported here in the context of the following caveats:

- The relatively small sample of subjects interviewed ($N = 82$) included 47 at a Carnegie 1 research university, which represents the most elite U.S. research institutions. The second site was a Carnegie 2 research university ($N = 16$), as was the third site ($N = 19$). Consequently, the findings cannot be generalized to other institutions. Given the small sample size (nine departments at three universities), the results may, at best, reflect the experiences of some of the female students and faculty at these research sites.

- The small number of graduate students ($N = 51$) does not permit a comparative analysis by field.

- The experiences reported by the respondents do not reflect those of racial/ethnic minorities (i.e., African Americans, Asians, and Hispanics).

- The lack of a matched sample of *male* graduate students and faculty restricts discussion of gender differences in school and career experiences. On the other hand, matching techniques can also distort comparisons, since the small number of women available for matching in a category may represent a higher ability level than the larger number of males (Etzkowitz et al., 1992).

- Although the interviewers are experienced researchers, the possibility of interviewer bias remains. Thus, although the traditional anthropological practice of same gender interviewing was followed, it is possible the interviewers' gender, race, or age could have affected the respondents' answer.

Despite these caveats, we believe that such a qualitative analysis enriches our understanding of some of the barriers that limit the full participation of women in academic science and engineering. Moreover, a recent review of research on women in science in the countries of the European Union and other international studies report similar findings (Talapessy, 1993). We are confident, therefore, that our research accurately reflects a chronic condition of sexual discrimination in academic science departments and an underlying culture that is hostile to women.

Barriers to Participation

Although there has been some recent progress, women continue to be chronically underrepresented in scientific careers and their participation declines as one ascends the career ladder (Zuckerman, Cole and Bruer, 1991). While scientific training is an arduous process for all aspirants, our research, and that of others, suggests that many women who aspire to scientific careers are blocked by a series of barriers that do not exist, in the same degree, for their male colleagues, and that many of those who succeed do so only by truly heroic efforts (Abir-Am and Outram, 1987).

There has been a general tendency to categorize the barriers that confront women in professions in two stages: (1) a threshold "beyond which gender no longer matters," and (2) a "glass ceiling of gender-specific obstacles to advancement into top positions." In the first, women encounter difficulties advancing in a field but the obstacles fall away once a certain status is attained; in the second, there is a particular career level women may attain at which point a blockage occurs to further advancement—for example, women are blocked from attaining full professorship in science departments at leading universities (Sonnert, 1990). The threshold effect presumes that women face barriers only in the early stages of their career, while the glass ceiling presumes barriers only at the higher levels of careers.

We find that women face barriers to entry and achievement on all rungs of the academic ladder. A series of mechanisms work against the progress of women in academic careers in science and engineering, including the advising system. There are also sources of subtle and not-so-subtle bias derived from the taken-for-granted male model of doing science that discourage women from full participation. Finally, there are such extra-academic factors as the different socialization of men and women and issues of marriage and family. These problems are often intertwined so that a phenomenon discussed in one category of analysis also surfaces in another. In our analysis, we discuss three types of barriers to entry into scientific careers: barriers that arise from (1) traditional socialization, (2) the structure of the academic system, and (3) discriminatory employment practices. We also suggest how these barriers can be eliminated or at least lowered.

The Structure of the Academic System

There is increasing recognition that the academic structure, rather than facilitating the passage of women, has mechanisms that actively push out large numbers of qualified and competent women (Matyas and Dix, 1992; Talapessy, 1993). The strength of these negative forces insures that only those with strongest motivation or financial resources succeed (Ruivo, 1987). Even those elements built into the system to assist students, such as an advisory system, sometimes fail to direct women toward progress to the degree.

In graduate school, students are expected to develop a close working relationship with their faculty advisor, a relationship that lasts several years and is crucial to the progress of the student through the program and out into the professional world. Previous researchers have identified negative interactional patterns in male advisors' relationships with their female graduate students that "lessen their opportunity for advancement" (Fox, 1989, p. 226). We found some instances where advising was based upon the faulty assumption that women had been socialized and educated the same as men. Further, some advisors simply could not take women seriously as graduate students because they perceived them to be less capable and uncompetitive.

Female experiences with male advisors range from denigrative to supportive. On the negative side are interactions that leave women with doubt about their self-worth. Even though this advisor probably thought that he was allaying concerns of his female advisee, the effect was the reverse: "He said to me, 'You don't have anything to worry about, they want women; so you'll pass [the qualifying exams].' . . . You have the feeling, 'Am I here because I'm a woman or because I am qualified?' It's like they take away all your achievements." Women also discussed specific negative incidents of gender-related presumptions of lack of scientific ability. For example, a female student was talking to a professor about her problems and he said she was an "emotional female." She comments: "Maybe he was thinking I shouldn't be in physics. I always thought he was a nice guy." Depending upon their awareness, sensitivity, and political stance on sex roles, male faculty can exacerbate or mitigate the effects of traditional female socialization. There appear to be two types of men in science with respect to women: (1) those who follow the male model, with negative consequences for women; and (2) those who are aware of the deleterious effect of the male model on women and who attempt to avert its worst consequences for their female advisees.

Most women are not socialized to understand the political strategies necessary to advance within the academic system. Without an advisor who is willing to be encouraging and directive, women are often unable to figure out the strategies necessary to get through graduate school. Women report that the best advisors are encouraging, give concrete directions, and show them the ropes. A woman faculty member explained that many women lacked a strategy to deal with the admissions process:

What you're supposed to do is get . . . the brochure and if you want to get in at least say that's what you want. The women don't seem to have grasped that. . . . The men go down the list and say, I want to work with this professor for this reason, that professor for that reason. . . . The females give me no indication that they have even looked at the brochure.

It is not only male advisors' treatment of female students that affects their situation, but also how male advisors instruct their male students to act toward women. A female graduate student said that "I hear rumors about myself. . . . [I heard that] a faculty member was advising his students that it might be interesting to have an affair with me."

These frequent negative instances are offset by occasions when men have served as successful advisors to women. A female student explained:

His attitude toward women is very understanding, very supportive, without being condescending. He doesn't say, "I understand what's going on," which is offensive because it's hard for a man to understand what's going on. He doesn't bring these issues up, I bring them up. He is very politically aware. He'll say, "Don't talk to ——." Sometimes [his advice] was because of sexism and sometimes because this person was an arrogant son-of-a-bitch and sometimes because this is a good person, but is just not comfortable with women.

Marriage and Family

A number of companies and government agencies report a series of interventions to reduce "work-family conflicts" but intervention models targeting women faculty are few in number for this or any other issue of concern to women in academic science (Matyas and Dix, 1992). Most notable is a "from the bottom up" electronic mail network of female computer scientists and engineers. In this network, topics such as work-family conflicts, increasing the number of women on review panels, and sexist advertising campaigns are discussed and, when appropriate, campaigns for change are organized (Goldman, 1993). From the top down, most notable is a series of NSF programs offering visiting professorships, research initiation awards, and mid-career research awards targeted at women. Nevertheless, the elements of an academic system that is hostile to women persist.

It is no surprise that pregnancy and childbearing still have negative consequences for women in the world of work in the United States (Gerson, 1985). However, the impacts appear to be especially strong in academic science, given its structural features that require virtually exclusive attention to research achievement during the years that coincide with fertility. Realization of what lies ahead sometimes deflects women from pursuing the Ph.D. A woman engineer speaking to a colloquium organized to encourage women students at a private research university to pursue engineering careers advised them to seek jobs in industry after the B.A. She pointed out that once they were established in their group, industry would accommodate part-time work or work at home during childbearing and early child-rearing years. She informed the audience that she chose not to pursue a Ph.D. because of her desire to have children before age thirty. At best, females have to calculate carefully how to integrate family and children with their scientific work; at worst, the inability to establish a balance drives them out of academic science.

Marriage and children appear to negatively impact women's careers in academic science at three key times: (1) pregnancy during graduate school, (2) marriage at the point of seeking a job, and (3) pregnancy prior to tenure. In addition, we found some disparagement of marriage during the graduate student career. Women, but not men, are sometimes thought to be less than serious about their science if they do not remain single while in graduate school. A female graduate student recalled: "When I first interviewed to come here, I was single. On my first day in the department, I had on an engagement ring. [My advisor's] attitude was 'families and graduate programs don't go together very well.' He was worried that I was going to blow my first year planning my wedding."

Women graduate students expect that they will be penalized for having children. Pregnancy is discouraged and graduate women who have children are encouraged to take leaves of absence that tend to become permanent withdrawals. In one department a faculty informant reported that only one of the students who had a child was left. The expectation that women students will succumb to the pressures of childbearing and child rearing makes some male and female faculty wary of taking on women students in the first place, especially since funding is tight and every place must be made to count. One female faculty member stated: "If a student had a baby with her, I wouldn't have her. Students who have babies here get no work done. It's not that I wouldn't take a woman with a child in the first place, but at the first sign of trouble, I would just tell her to leave. If my students fail, it looks bad for me."

One department made an attempt to take childbearing into account in its evaluation process. A female student explained: "If a Ph.D. [student] has a child, she will be given some leeway for that semester . . . [but] it's such a small amount of time. I think women should get . . . at least a year." In most of the departments we studied, there was a strong bias against women combining parenthood with a graduate career. Most advisors simply expect female students to delay having children until after the degree.

Tenure

The dissonance between the tenure clock and the biological clock for women once again illustrates that the career structure of science is compatible with traditional assumptions of *male* youthful achievement. This is taken for granted. Despite the paucity of evidence for an association of youth with scientific achievement (Merton, 1973a), the academic system is geared toward a forced march in the early years, only allowing a slower pace later. This is exactly the opposite of a structure that would be compatible for most women.

The incompatibility of the seven-year race for tenure with the biological clock for childbearing has obvious negative consequences for women's participation in high-powered academic science. A male faculty member told us that if women would wait until after age thirty-five to have children, there would be no problem. They would be able to pursue tenure single-mindedly without interference from other obligations. He recognized that most women were unwilling to delay having children that long and thus saw no answer to this dilemma.

A graduate of this program, now a professor at another university, reflected upon the relationship between the biological and the tenure clocks. In discussing her plans for having children, she said: "I would feel much more confidence if I had tenure but I would be 38 and I don't choose to have a child that late." One female faculty member reported that her tenure review has caused an added measure of anxiety. She said: "When it comes to the real facts, that's when you feel discrimination. The pregnancy worries me. It's always the wrong moment. It puts you on a slower track. If the baby hadn't shown up, I would have pushed for an early decision. Now I will wait." Career disruptions are often caused by the inability of the academic system to easily allow a modest reduction in workload. A total temporary withdrawal is often the only option, but then the expected return sometimes does not happen.

Departmental and university-wide efforts to make workplace child care facilities more widely available would help. An infant care center in a neighboring school, discovered by one female graduate student, made a significant difference in the ability of several women with children in one department to carry on their graduate work virtually without interruption. The center, which cares for children from ten weeks to three years of age, was an experimental site with a capacity of eight children. Although there are a few other facilities for older children affiliated with the university or located in the neighborhood, child care is still a major concern for parents. This area of concern has received more attention from companies than from universities in recent years (Matyas and Dix, 1992).

If the policy objective is to significantly increase the number of women pursuing high-powered scientific careers, institutional accommodations will have to be made for women who wish to combine family with career. Achieving equality is not just a matter of opening up opportunities but of changing the structure of the academic system. Simply put, women are more vulnerable than men prior to tenure. Accommodation for time conflicts must be made for women faculty members with children. Women who wish to pursue traditional female roles along with a scientific career must be accommodated by allowing a longer time span before the tenure decision. This accommodation had been promised to one faculty member in our sample but subsequently was not allowed.

Efforts at reforming the academic structure by reducing the "time bind" for women are fraught with danger, as arguments on behalf of change are often turned into negative reflections on women's scientific abilities. Even in the absence of accommodation to their needs, the relatively few women in the system have maintained their productivity (Zuckerman, Cole, and Bruer, 1991). One female professor has spoken up in faculty meetings on behalf of extending the time before tenure review for women with children. She sees this recommendation as a double-edged sword. For example, pressuring for reduced demands on women with children might jeopardize their status by supporting the notion that women with children cannot be productive. Of course, the extension could be made gender-neutral, with the same provisions offered to men with extensive responsibilities for child rearing.

Socialization

Graduate students are expected to work independently—and to fashion a strategy for personal success independently. Interpersonal support is scarce or nonexistent. These expectations are antithetical to those generated by traditional female socialization. In addition, the needs of women, based on socialization that encourages supportive interaction with teachers, are frowned upon by many male and some female faculty as indicative of inability. As a female graduate student put it: "The men have the attitude of 'Why should people need their hands held?' " Lack of a supportive environment exacerbates problems of often already low levels of self-confidence.

Beyond cumulative disadvantage carried over from previous negative experiences lies the realm of "marginal disadvantage," the cuts and stigmatizing reproaches experienced in graduate school. These range from assumptions of devalued admission to simply not having one's comments in a research group meeting taken seriously, only to hear them repeated a few minutes later, in a more confident voice, by a male counterpart, with acceptance the final outcome. Disadvantage experienced at the margin of presumed success, after admission to a prestigious graduate program, is the unkindest cut of all. The fall to failure from such a lofty height is brought about in many ways.

The devaluation of women's scientific contributions has been found to be widespread (Benjamin, 1991). It takes many forms, including crediting the male partner in scientific collaborations and ignoring the work of women (Scott, 1990). At our primary research site, despite a formal and even at times a strongly stated commitment to nondiscriminatory treatment of women, discrimination was manifested informally. For example, a female graduate student reported differential treatment of men's and women's contributions. She said: "In group meetings, I get the sense that if a woman says something, 'okay, fine,' and that's the end of that." Women feel their contributions are ignored.

Sometimes women are devalued by not being included in events. A female graduate student reported that invisibility was imposed on her when "you have a visitor to the lab, and the professor introduces the male students, but not you."

Women found it difficult to be taken seriously as professionals outside the department as well. One said: "When I go to conferences and ask a question, the answer gets addressed to a man in the room. It's worse in physics than in other fields." A female graduate student reported her response to being ignored: "It's always a thing where, being invisible, you don't exist. . . . It was, in a sense, that I didn't exist." Other times, women are made to feel different by being given excessive visibility. A female graduate student reported that a professor was "addressing the class, 'Gentlemen' . . . and then made a big pause and looked at me and added, 'and lady.' I was different. Other people noticed it." At still other times, women are patronized. A female graduate student commented: "I was sitting at the table and he kept referring to us as 'my girls.' In that context I didn't like it. He was thinking of us differently. He didn't say, 'my boys.' "

Many women come into graduate programs in science with a low degree of self-confidence. Women in physics, chemistry, and computer science reported that their graduate school experience further eroded their self-confidence. The comments of one female graduate student are instructive: "Women couch their words with all these qualifiers [because they are so insecure] . . . 'I'm not sure, but maybe.'. . . My science is different because of my socialization, not my gender."

If things are working out well, the initial lack of self-confidence is not too important, but if problems arise, then negative feelings come forth. For example, one woman had this to say: "It is much worse if a woman fails an exam because her self-confidence is so low. I got an A− on an exam and was upset. The man sitting next to me got a C and he said, 'So what?' " Finally, if the barriers remain high, low self-confidence translates into an increased rate of attrition. This failure of retention can be viewed as a result of an accumulative thwarting of the development of a viable professional identity. Even those who do not give up, or are not pushed out, often reduce their professional aspirations.

Employment

Given the mismatch between traditional academic culture and female gender, it is not surprising that most scientists and engineers come from a relatively small segment of the population (U.S. Congress, 1991). At a time when women constitute 51 percent of the total population and 45 percent of the total work force, they constitute only 16 percent of all scientists and engineers employed in the United States (NSF, 1992c). Moreover, among trained scientists, females scientists are more likely than their male counterparts to be unemployed, underemployed, or holders of part-time jobs.

In our study, we have identified several patterns of impediment at the point of the job search, including one of deferring to a male partner, and a less usual one of ignoring personal considerations. Departments also typically make hiring decisions differentially by gender: they consider women's personal obligations to spouses and children while ignoring them for men. The assumption, of course, is that women will be strongly affected by their ties; men less so. A certain personal strict adherence to a rigid academic career path and total time commitment are among the unstated requirements for many jobs.

The highest climbers on the academic ladder of success are able to accept the most promising and prestigious postdoctoral and faculty positions without regard to any other consideration. This process has disastrous career consequences for women who are unable or unwilling to make individualistic locational decisions. As one observer put it: "The academic market is a national one. Those who do not accommodate their choice of geographical location and willingness to move for their careers may lose out" (Rosenfeld, 1984, p. 99).

Marriage and children are generally viewed by male faculty members as impediments to a scientific career for women. Even those male faculty members most supportive of women acknowledge having had some disappointments with women who settled for jobs that were not commensurate with their achievements. These are jobs that men of accomplishment would not accept. One male faculty member commented: "You have some extremely good people you think are going to go out and make a mark and then somehow or other they marry somebody and spend their time in a bad career." For a man to decide not to take his career seriously is like admitting he takes drugs. For a woman to say she puts her family ahead of her career is considered a virtue; the pressures are all in that direction. Far too often, women are praised for sacrificing their career in favor of their husbands. Pressures to do so come from society, from relatives, and to some extent from the men involved or the parents of the husband.

A few women take a different tack by willingly breaking off personal relationships that interfere with accepting the best possible job. A male professor portrayed the situation of a woman who was involved in a relationship:

I asked her, "To what extent is his career going to interact with what you do?" She said, "Not at all. I want to find the best job I can and if it works out for him, O.K., and if it doesn't, well then that's the end of the relationship." She's at [prestigious Eastern university] and he's still out in ——, so that's the end of him. She took what I would say is a typically man's approach to things, that the career is the primary decision, but they don't all do that.

Geographical Mobility

A typical scenario that has been identified is a woman marrying a man in the same field who completes his graduate work first. He finds the best job he can without geographical constraints. When the woman finishes, she finds what job she can in a circumscribed region (Max, 1982). Women who are already married often select their graduate school based on what is available in a region and choose a job based on similar considerations. Second-rank research universities attract many higher quality candidates than they might otherwise, due to women's geographical restrictions.

The limited geographical mobility that many women face can be addressed in at least two ways:

1. Hiring both husband and wife, even in the same department, taking account of the fact that graduate students in the same discipline and department often marry.

2. Relaxing formal and/or informal prohibitions against hiring one's own graduates.

Universities are seldom eager to hire both husband and wife in the same department. The departmental work site tends to become a place where graduate students find marriage partners. At the time of our study, one department was conducting a search for a chair, and the leading candidate's wife was seeking a position at a junior level. Even though she was regarded as eminently qualified for a position that was available in her area and the administration was willing to approve both hirings, faculty members' objections to bringing in both overrode all other considerations. Whenever specific objections were taken into account, such as removing the chair from oversight of review decisions concerning his wife by sending them directly to the dean, new objections were raised. The departmental culture was resistant to accommodating a dual-career family. Department members believed that a married couple would bring a heightened level of personal relationships into the department and that this would be inevitably disruptive, beyond the usual friendship patterns and cliques of academic life.

As more men are married to women whose careers are important to them, male geographical mobility will also be affected. As both men and women face geographical constraints on their job choices, we can predict that the link between career success and ability to change work site will be weakened. Departments that made exceptions and hired their own female graduates provided a significant and at times essential career boost for women who otherwise might have been shunted aside from research careers in academia due to locational constraint.

"Male" and "Female" Models of Science

Essentially, women are expected to follow a "male model" of academic success that includes a total time commitment to scientific work and aggressive competitive relations with peers. There are two contrasting "ideal typical" responses to this situation by female graduate students and faculty members: (1) women who follow the male model and expect other women to do so; and (2) women who attempt to delineate an alternative model, allowing for a balance between work and private spheres.

Relatively few women are willing to adapt to the male model of academic science, which involves an aggressive, competitive stance and an unconditional devotion to work, at least until tenure. We call the female scientists who follow this route "instrumentals." Most women attempt to define a women's academic model, balancing work and nonwork roles, with an emphasis by faculty members on cooperation at the work site among members of their research group (Kemelgor, 1989). These women we call "balancers."

Instrumentals

Instrumentals are able to act independently and strategically. A female faculty member described her strategy for getting through graduate school: "I specifically chose the chair as my advisor because I wanted to graduate. . . . He had a reputation for graduating all his students. I knew I was doing well when I picked that guy. [His research area] didn't matter so much. The research I wanted to do, I could do after I graduated." Instrumentals typically view the academic system as favorable to women. A female graduate student who believed in doing "the politically right thing" said: "Physics is incredibly biased in favor of women. They work much harder to keep the female students . . . [because] most don't come in with adequate preparation. There are women who talk themselves out of taking the qualifying exams." This individual was outwardly hostile toward women, favoring the men whom she emulated: "I worked through my undergraduate career by myself. The women don't have enough intelligence to work things out for themselves." However, she also noted the debilitating effects of traditional socialization on women: "The guys have more . . . self-confidence. Women end up getting help, and then they end up in graduate schools they wouldn't normally get into and they're stuck because it is built into them to get assistance."

Instrumentals are willing to put in night and weekend work hours, making the lab the center of their social as well as work life. One such woman faculty member said: "It never occurs to the males that they could come in at 9 and leave at 5, five days a week, and get a Ph.D. They're here at 3 A.M., weekends. You never see a woman here off hours. You see all the males."

Instrumentals are typically unmarried or divorced and without responsibilities for child rearing. An informant noted that "a common pattern is that women who are successful are single or divorced and dedicate most of their energy to their career." They are often ambivalent toward women students who are not as directed as they are. A female faculty member said: "Males come to me immediately with a problem. Women muddle off. I try cajoling them, pleading with them, yelling at them."

Balancers

In contrast to the instrumentals, balancers find the highly competitive nature of academic science to be problematic since it conflicts with their own preference for cooperation, as described by this student: "Given the competitiveness that goes on around here, it is a lot harder to be open, honest, and supportive because you don't know if you are going to get turned on."

The current constrained funding climate exacerbates women's unstable position, causing faculty who are fearful of productivity losses to be less willing to tolerate deviation from the traditional male model of doing science. Despite these obstacles, a new scientific work role is emerging as women and men both struggle to restructure traditional family and work roles (Gerson, 1985). To treat the lab strictly as a work site is a necessary strategy for women (and some men) who want to be highly productive as scientists and yet maintain an outside life. These faculty members had a commitment to raising children and interacting with their family that was equal in importance to their work commitment.

The balancers wish to pursue multiple roles, typically family and work, seeking a reasonable division between the two spheres. They organize their laboratories on a collegial, noncompetitive basis, and they try to keep close to normal business hours, resuming intellectual work at home after their children are asleep. Balancers also adopt a nonhovering management style that allows their students considerable leeway and initiative in order to keep their scientific life from becoming an all-consuming activity. Despite this effort, some female students felt that their mentors were not spending enough time with their children and questioned whether they would be willing to make such a choice in order to pursue a high-powered academic career.

Perhaps ironically, multiple roles have recently become accepted for high-status males in science who wish to combine participation in entrepreneurial ventures with the professorial role (Etzkowitz, 1989). However, combining the professorial role with serious attention to family obligations is seldom an acceptable stance for a high level career in academic science or other professions (Fox and Hesse-Biber, 1984). Informal activities outside the department are also often linked to traditional sex role activities and venues. In one department in a related study, a regular pick-up basketball game was a site for exchange of informal comments on research activities, along with visits to a male-oriented local bar. Inevitably a female faculty member felt excluded from "the club" (Kemelgor, 1989).

Some women were able to work out an accommodation with the demands of a career at a research university by strictly budgeting their work time and making every minute of it count. For these women, the university was solely a work site, not combining with it a social environment. For many males, the time put in at the lab is not all work related, but being in the lab extremely long hours is part of the accepted persona of the successful academic scientist. The balancing stance is not solely a female response to academia. Some male faculty adopted this position to a limited extent but typically admitted that their participation in domestic life and child rearing was less than their spouse's. Moreover, not all women who wished to balance the demands of an academic research career and family were able to achieve this goal. Graduate students who were encouraged to take leaves after a pregnancy often did not return. Women interested in academic research careers often decided to accept industry positions either to give their husband first preference in a job search or to have a work role that was explicitly limited to a 9-to-5 commitment. Some junior faculty members abandoned research careers to accept positions in teaching colleges. Thus, at present, the strategy of balancing career and family is contrary to the culture of high-status research universities and is difficult to arrange and sustain. However, this is the option that most women in our sample wished to pursue.

Departmental Reform

The tendency to focus on individual women and their problems in studying the status of women in science can divert attention from the way that Ph.D. programs are organized and from issues of structural reform (Matyas, 1993). When the German-style hierarchical professorship failed to take hold as the model for organizing research and teaching in U.S. universities in the late nineteenth century, the department was invented as a consortium of equals, more or less (Oleson and Voss, 1979). The U.S. academic model was based upon a professorial status, with the ability to initiate research, granted early in the academic career. Research was built up relatively inexpensively by hiring students as research assistants instead of using senior personnel, as in the traditional German model.

In the last fifty years, the Ph.D. training process in the sciences was also transformed from an individualized research process to a group research effort in which younger students build upon older students' work (Etzkowitz, 1992). Under these conditions the dissertation has also been transformed, becoming less close in form to a book and more like a series of articles on discrete topics. Some women assume that the old model still holds. Often less integrated into their research group than men, they are likely to expect to have to produce a magnum opus for a dissertation. Some male faculty, resistant to women, use this cultural lag against their female students by assigning macroscopic projects in expectation of inducing failure. We now examine some of the major strategies that have been proposed to improve the condition of women in science at the graduate level: role modeling, critical mass, and structural reform.

Role Models

Previous research has identified the characteristics of successful women role models who integrated "professional and personal concerns" (Mokros, Erkut, and Spichiger, 1981, p. 11). Beyond strictly professional issues, women mentees are concerned with the interpersonal quality of the relationship and seek a sympathetic mentor (Dowdall and Boneparth, 1979).

In the sciences, male senior researchers have traditionally served as role models for their junior colleagues. As women entered scientific careers, they were expected to follow a male model, accept a distinctly subordinate status (the scientific equivalent of the traditional female role, the research associate), or leave the profession. Recently, some women have attempted to carve out a new status and a new professional identity for themselves in the world of academic science (Kemelgor, 1989). Female graduate students prefer to have a range of models of female behaviors in science available to emulate. At present, the numbers of female faculty are so small that there are often few or even no choices of role models. A female junior faculty member described her role model in graduate school: "Another woman did quite well. . . . It showed it was possible. There were a number of women in my field who were well known as I was going through; most of them were single."

Most women graduate students made a sharp distinction between women faculty whom they viewed as positive or negative as role models. Women faculty who were perceived to be instrumentals were often not viewed as viable models. On the other hand, a woman faculty member who was successfully balancing career and family was looked to as a model by several women in her department, even though she was somewhat less available due to time constraints. A female graduate student said: "[She] is a role model precisely because she can balance the two. When you do find the time to finally meet with her, you have her attention."

The need for women faculty to show how professional and family responsibilities could both be met was expressed by a student who said: "I think it would be interesting to see [the female professor] get pregnant, so we could see how someone else deals with the situation. I have no clue whatsoever." For the most part, female students are left to feel they must be pioneers. In some instances, this situation was resented. The few who felt they did have role models identified them as being from high school, undergraduate school, or industry—or they were their mothers.

Most importantly, the role model women wanted was the woman who could concretely explain the necessary strategies and steps to be taken to succeed in graduate school. This conclusion derives from the reality that

(1) rules are made by men; (2) young men have been socialized to those rules and are further socialized in graduate school, and they have learned the strategies; (3) most women have not been socialized to be autonomous, and therefore they have difficulty figuring out the rules; and (4) most male advisors do not teach women the strategies necessary to succeed.

Of course, this finding does not hold for those very few graduate women who excluded other interests in favor of their career. The absence of viable female role models in most of the departments studied creates anxiety among female graduate students and is believed by them to contribute to the rate of attrition. Nevertheless, female graduate students report successful and unsuccessful experiences with both male and female advisors. Men can be sensitive advisors and women can be relevant role models, but few men and women faculty currently meet the needs of most women graduate students.[4] Women graduate students seek out women faculty members as advisors in hopes of finding a sympathetic mentor, while male graduate students sign up with a woman only after she has achieved a distinguished position in the field. The key to mentoring women is not whether the mentors are women or men, but whether they are able to relate to women.

Critical Mass

The relative lack of women in senior positions in academic science departments has been found to leave female junior faculty and graduate students feeling isolated, without the necessary support to build a successful career. One solution that has been proposed is not to hire a few token role models but to achieve "critical mass" for women in every department. Despite the distance from this goal (many computer science departments, for example, do not have a single female faculty member), we suggest that this worthy goal is a necessary but insufficient condition to achieve parity for women in academic science.

Women faculty in a department seldom constitute a homogeneous group. Instrumentals may act even more negatively and be less sensitive to female students than male faculty members who are aware of women's issues. The presence of several women in a department faculty may not, in itself, be sufficient to overcome barriers to female students and will not even provide many of them with relevant role models, if they are primarily instrumentals. Nevertheless, the "critical mass" thesis of having several women on the faculty of a science department remains to be seriously tested, especially in departments in the physical sciences and engineering that likely have no senior women and may even have no women on their faculty. Even when "instrumentals" and "balancers" are at odds with each other, these contrasting models at least provide women students with a range of possibilities to choose among to integrate into their own stance.

Structural Reform

Rather than particular measures targeted at women, the departmental structure could be the most important reform. We have identified two contrasting Ph.D. formats: a "weeding out" and a "member of the family" approach. In the former model, each step of the Ph.D. process is viewed as an opportunity to decide whether the candidate should proceed to the next step; the assumption is that a larger number of persons have been admitted than are actually worthy of achieving the degree. In this type of program, deselection or "weeding out" is normative. In the latter model, the critical decision point is viewed as having been made during the admissions process; all who have been selected to enter the program are deemed worthy of earning the Ph.D. degree. Only exceptional circumstances should displace anyone from being a "member of the family." In one chemistry program, the dissertation was defined as the publishable papers that a student had written during a given time span of the degree program (Etzkowitz, 1992). In a physics program, research accomplishments were viewed as an acceptable justification for relaxing the standard for passing qualifying exams.

One department had undergone significant change with respect to its treatment of women. Among its leaders were several middle-aged males who had simultaneously been in therapy in a community where the local culture had been strongly influenced by feminist values. In this context, one man pointed out that they were being unconsciously dismissive of the work of a female faculty member up for tenure. They reviewed their behavior and decided to change their attitudes and practices.[5] They also revised the departmental structure to emphasize collegiality and gender-blind decision making.

All the female students and faculty reported that they had joined this department rather than another prestigious one because of their perception that it offered a collaborative, cooperative, and collegial milieu. They were attracted by the warm interpersonal interactions experienced when they interviewed and by a sense of personal concern for the candidate conveyed by faculty and students. Most had been disturbed by the demoralization of students at other departments where they had interviewed, having heard stories of exploitative advisors and anonymity in large research groups.

In this department, a female academic model based on interpersonal relationships, affiliation, and nurturance had become accepted as legitimate and had even become the departmental norm. This was in strong contrast to another research site, where the expression by women of a need for these characteristics in the laboratory environment was derided as a desire for dependence and emotionality by the adherents of the patriarchal system that was in place. The context into which reforms are introduced is critical to their acceptance; the culture and organization of departments play an important role in whether reforms will be accepted or rejected.

Administrative Actions

It is clear that administrative actions, even if they do not change attitudes, can affect behavior. A female graduate dean at another university reported on the efficacy at her institution of administrative leadership to remind people of gender and minority issues at every step of the academic process. Occasionally, university administrators take direct measures to encourage the development of critical mass by offering to make positions available if women or minority faculty can be recruited.

Academic administrators may be unaware of problems at the departmental level. The affirmative action officer at the primary research site reported that she received virtually no complaints from women in the science and engineering departments, while there were many from the humanities and social sciences. She presumed that the universalistic spirit of science, rather than an environment that suppresses the expression of gender differences, was responsible for the paucity of complaints. In one instance, a female graduate student contemplated making a complaint against a male faculty member who was discussing pornographic images on a computer screen with his male graduate student. The incident took place in her presence in an office that she shared with the male graduate student. She refrained from making an official complaint, fearful of endangering her degree. However, the matter attained sufficient visibility within the department that the chair sent out a strongly worded message condemning the practice as unacceptable and warning against its repetition. Although the chair's response to this incident was publicized on the departmental and nationwide women-in-computer-science e-mail network, the department remained basically unchanged in its treatment of female graduate students.

Industry

The pressures of the tenure decision lead many women to seek more stable, less pressured careers in industrial research. Industry has established numerous programs to attract and retain women in recent years (Matyas and Dix, 1992). Motivated in some instances by the desire to obtain military contracts (one of the few areas in which federal affirmative action laws were seriously enforced in the 1980s), this effort falls short.

Many companies still have problems with accepting women's technical contributions and with promoting women to positions of responsibility (Matyas and Dix, 1992). Despite a "'company climate' that is often not as supportive of women employees as it could be" (Matyas and Dix, 1992, p. 86), an industrial career appears increasingly attractive to women scientists and engineers who wish to balance a professional and a private life.

Regardless of department, most women graduate students reported that they intended to pursue an industrial career because it was more compatible with family life. One informant concluded: "Women will go into industry. It's 9 to 5. It's more flexible. They have daycare and childcare. There are federal rules they have to abide by. . . . The support systems exist [in industry] and it's the only way you can [have a family]."

For some women, the experience of working in industry while they were pursuing the Ph.D. had a very positive effect. They found that their technical work was accepted and rewarded, which built their self-confidence. This positive experience in industry led them to pursue their doctorates with increased self-confidence.

A program for women in science sponsored by AT&T is especially significant in this regard (Morrison, 1992). The company offers fellowships to a highly select group of women to support their graduate studies. It also provides them with mentors and summer employment opportunities at AT&T. However, we found that possibly the greatest contribution of this program to women's success in attaining the Ph.D. was its mentoring process. When women encountered difficulties in graduate studies, they were able to get support from their industry mentors that made a crucial difference to their graduate careers (Etzkowitz, 1993).

When AT&T scientists visited their female mentee's university for other reasons, they would stop by and have a conversation with her faculty advisor. A positive evaluation of the proposed research often had the effect of allowing her dissertation to go forward. Sometimes additional steps were necessary. For example, when an advisor would not agree to support a student's work in the university, an informal arrangement was made for the Ph.D. student to complete her dissertation research under supervision at Bell Labs. An industrial point of reference for women graduate students can provide a valuable counterpoint to academia—especially if their industrial mentors are willing to intervene on their behalf when necessary.

Government

Debates on a domestic shortage of scientific personnel focus on the underrepresentation of women in science, even as increasing immigration of scientists shifts the balance between national and international interests. Irrespective of the issue of shortages are the requirements of equity (see

Chapter 8 below). An occupational structure, with highly distorted rates of participation from different segments of the population that depend on extensive public support, is most fully legitimated when it draws upon the entire population and all regions of the country. Laws prohibiting discrimination are on the books, and although they apply to academia, they are seldom vigorously enforced (Carson and Chubin, 1992).

During the 1980s, the federal government withdrew from most of its efforts at reducing gender discrimination at universities. Many academic scientists and engineers are aware that the Defense Department's strong interest in military contractors hiring women made a significant difference. Indeed, a dean of engineering proudly pointed this out as an instance of women's advancement in engineering. But when asked if the same measure could be applied to the academic environment with similar results, he expressed a lack of interest in the experiment. Certainly, a reinvigorated affirmative action effort and enforcement of existing federal laws could make an important difference to the advancement of women in science (Chubin and Robinson, 1992).

Conclusion

The succession of impediments to the entry of women into scientific careers that narrows the stream to an extremely small flow at the stage of graduate training has been conceptualized as cumulative disadvantage. Even given these disadvantages, however, a significant number of women receive degrees in science at the B.A. and even the Ph.D. levels. Nevertheless, fewer women pursue careers in science than men, and there are few senior women professors (Moen, 1988). The disadvantages that accumulate to narrow the flow into the science career pipeline are supplemented by additional disadvantages, at the margin, that discourage even the most highly motivated women who have taken steps to pursue scientific and engineering careers at the doctoral level.

Removal of some or all of these barriers at the doctoral and junior and senior faculty levels could, in the short term, increase women's participation in science and engineering. Taking such steps could also provide role models to assist in long-term efforts to lower barriers at the early stages of the life course, thereby increasing the flow of women into the science career pipeline.

Female graduate students and professors, after successfully negotiating the numerous barriers to entry that exclude so many other women, often pursue less demanding careers than their male peers. These women are not lost to science. Rather they are women who, with a few exceptions, are excluded from positions in the top academic departments in their field.

Many pursue research careers in industry; others have taken appointments in teaching colleges. Whether these scientists are excluded from high-level academic careers through discrimination by academic departments unwilling to accept women as equals or other reasons, the result is the same. There is a pool of female scientists working in industry and lower down the academic ladder whom their advisors, usually men, agree are the equal of their male peers who are pursuing research careers at the highest academic levels. If professorial jobs were made available, qualified women scientists could be recruited to create a critical mass of at least three women in each leading academic department. This would provide the range of female role models necessary to bring forth a large next generation of women scientists.

Luce professorships and the NSF visiting professorships for women (VPW) program provide individual permanent and temporary positions, but no program is yet available of the magnitude to create by itself a critical mass. However, an internal university commitment can provide the necessary scale of resources for achieving a critical mass at least in some departments, as in the molecular biology department that we studied. A more radical suggestion, given the success of women's colleges in encouraging women's participation in science at the undergraduate level, is the development of graduate departments at some of these same institutions.

Such a bold step would provide a place for faculty to set an example of women organizing research groups that function collegially, effectively, and differently than the male model. Serious consideration of such a course of action might lead existing graduate programs to reevaluate their treatment of women, since the resources to initiate this reform of the academic system could well be drawn from the National Science Foundation, the National Institutes of Health, and other agencies that support existing graduate programs.

Specific steps could be taken to mitigate the negative effects of the male scientific ethos on the recruitment of women to science and engineering. The rigidity of the existing academic structure and male faculty misperceptions of female scientists constitute formidable barriers to the entry and retention of women at the highest levels of academic science. However, the fact that qualified women who would be interested in academic research careers are now in industry or in teaching colleges suggests that, should these final barriers be lowered or removed, women scientists who already exist might pursue careers at the highest levels of academic science.

The organization and culture of academic science deter many women of high scientific ability from making their contribution. In those instances where a department faced this situation and altered its behavior, women's participation improved dramatically. A broader recognition of the need to change and of the requisite actions is required to reconstruct male-gendered science and engineering departments.[6] Based on Linda Wilson's comments (in Mervis, 1992) and our analysis of the experience of female graduate students and faculty in the sciences and engineering, we make the following recommendations to increase women's participation in academic science and engineering:

- Acceptance of a female model of doing science in a collegial workplace accompanied by time for a private sphere of life apart from science;
- Synchronizing women's biological and tenure clocks by allowing a longer time span before tenure;
- Provision of a significant number of relevant role models so that younger women can envision a future in science.

Many scientists (male and female), scientific societies (e.g., Sigma Xi, AAAS), and funding agencies (e.g., NSF, NIH) are beginning to promote an alternative model that will enhance women's full participation in the scientific community. They raise equity issues in the face of strongly held beliefs on the part of many male scientists that the existing system produces an adequate number of female scientists. By accepting various parochial ways of conceptualizing, investigating, and organizing the conduct of science, significant sectors of the population have been excluded from full participation, and alternative cognitive perspectives and organizational styles have been repressed. As we become aware of such factors as masculine models of gender as the basis for many modes of doing science, a policy space is opened up where change can take place. Social movements and support groups organized by excluded groups, changes in departmental practices and university policies initiated by faculty and administrators, and governmental affirmative action policies and funding programs are all part of the emerging picture of science open to all talent, in fact as well as by precept.

Questions of gender and science have come into the foreground in sociological theory, feminist research, and human resource policy (Abir-Am, 1991). The sociology of science is moving beyond comparing male and female scientists according to implicitly masculine criteria, which have themselves come into question. Hypercompetitiveness has been attacked as counterproductive to "good science" (Mervis, 1992). The definition of research achievement in terms of number of publications, with article counts accepted as a primary indicator of productivity and achievement, is ambiguous. Women publish less frequently than men but their publications are more frequently cited (Long, 1990). This finding suggests different gender styles of scientific work, with women taking a more measured approach to research. Women appear to work more intensively on a subject before making their work public.

Norms of science that incorporate both traditional male and female perspectives into a broader nonsexist framework would free both experimentation and verification of knowledge from the exclusionary oppositions in which that which defines *feminine* is automatically antithetical to "good science" (Keller, 1986). Under these conditions, with impersonal evaluation a component of the social structure of science, we could experience as reality Maria Mitchell's exhortation that "no woman should say, 'I am but a woman!' But, a woman! What more could you ask to be" (Enna, 1993)?

Notes

A different version of this chapter appeared in *Science and Public Policy* (1992) as "Athena Unbound: Barriers to Women in Academic Science and Engineering." We wish to acknowledge the support of this research by the National Science Foundation Sociology Program Grant #SES-8913525 and by a visiting professorship award to SUNY Stony Brook from the Provost of the State University of New York.

1. At this university, the computer science department is located jointly in the Engineering School and the Faculty of Arts and Sciences.

2. The physics department at this university previously had two tenured women, one now emerita and the other deceased.

3. Since physics students are not assigned a faculty advisor until after they have completed two years, advisor data were missing for those who dropped out of the program before this point. In electrical engineering, dropout data were provided only for the prior year and did not include students who left after failing a qualifying exam administered after their first few months in the program.

4. In the four departments at private research universities, 22 percent of the female students have female faculty advisors; only 4 percent of the male students do. While the proportion of female and male students entering subfields where female faculty advisors are available is fairly similar (32 and 24 percent, respectively), the proportion actually signing up with those female professors differs by a factor of four (68 to 17 percent).

5. In another instance, change came only after a female faculty member threatened to resign when a sexist male faculty member was about to be named permanent chair. This action received national publicity, forcing university officials to do something about the sexist environment of the department. They prescribed a year of gender sensitivity training for the acting chair, who then resigned the position.

6. Indeed, the experience of the In-balance Program at the Center for Particle Astrophysics, University of California, Berkeley, indicates that many of these changes are necessary for both women and men.

CHAPTER 4

The Contributions of Historically Black Colleges and Universities to the Production of African American Scientists and Engineers

William Trent and John Hill

The 1969 annual meeting of the American Council on Education had as its theme "the campus and the racial crisis." The Council focused on the racial crisis on college campuses emerging, in part, both from successful efforts (following the passage of the 1964 Civil Rights Act) to increase minority student participation and from increased enrollment of African American students following the civil disturbances that erupted in 1965 and 1968. Nearly twenty years later, in 1987, the Council convened a special meeting in response to the declining participation of minority individuals in higher education, again with a particular focus on African American participation. African American enrollment in higher education had more than doubled from 1964 to 1969, increasing from 234,000 to 492,000, and by 1976 had exceeded one million. Prior to the 1960s and throughout the changes over the past two decades, it has been the historically black colleges and universities (HBCUs) that have sustained African American participation in higher education. While most of the increase in enrollment cited above is attributable to increased enrollment in traditionally white colleges and universities (TWCUs), it remains true today that HBCUs contribute a disproportionately larger number of earned degrees to African American citizens than either the number or the history of these colleges and universities would predict. Generally, the role of HBCUs in the production of African American degree recipients has largely supplied the intellectual talent that has enabled progress in dismantling segregation and furthering this nation's social agenda. Specifically, African American participation in the natural sciences and technical fields and professions has been substantially sustained by the efforts of HBCUs from 1976 through 1989.

In this chapter we examine degree recipients in science and engineering and also discuss the relative efficiency of HBCUs in converting freshman enrollments into degree recipients. This analysis adds to the growing body of studies that underscore the importance of HBCUs in the production of African Americans with bachelor's and higher degrees in science and engineering fields. The definition of science and engineering fields (S/E) includes the natural sciences, social and behavioral sciences, and engineering (health fields are not included in this analysis).

Data

Data were derived from the Higher Education General Information Surveys (HEGIS) and its successor, the Integrated Postsecondary Educational Data System (IPEDS) on enrollment and degree attainment for selected years covering the period 1976–89. These data report national enrollment and earned degree data by race at two-year intervals, beginning in 1975–76, the first year for which these data are available by race. These surveys provide institutional level data rather than student level data. This limits the analysis to reporting summary figures for individual schools or groups of schools rather than students.

Historical Background

The HBCUs were founded during a period of legal segregation to aid a population that lived under severe legal, economic, educational, political, and social restrictions in the United States (Anderson, 1988). Of the more than 150 colleges founded for the purpose of educating African Americans during legal segregation, there are 106 in existence today. (The list of HBCUs used in this study is from the U.S. Department of Education, White House Initiative Office.) Most of these institutions are located in the southern and border states. There are slightly more colleges under private (55) than public control (51), but the larger public institutions account for three-fourths of the enrollment in the HBCUs. Most of the HBCUs offer baccalaureate or higher degrees; there are only 19 two-year colleges.

In general, HBCUs have served as the principal conduit for the education of African Americans. This is especially the case for scientists and engineers; without these institutions, their number would be negligible. Just twenty years ago,

only 2 percent of this country's practicing physicians [were] black. The proportion of attorneys [was] extremely unequal: one for every 750 whites, but only one black attorney for every 5,000 blacks. . . . But without Meharry and Howard, the record would be unimaginably worse. . . . The Carnegie Commission on Higher Education reports that in 1968–69, out of 35,000 M.D. candidates in the nation, 393 were at Howard and 269 at Meharry. Less than 1 percent of the students in other medical schools were black. . . . Out of 15,408 dental students enrolled, 136 were at Meharry and 310 were at Howard. Only 21 of 50 dental schools, other than Howard and Meharry had any black students, and most of these had only one. (Watson, 1972, p. 6)

While their proportional contribution to the production of African American holders of the bachelor's and higher degrees has changed substantially since desegregation, the centrality of HBCUs has continued.

At the undergraduate level, the 80 HBCUs that offer bachelor's degrees provided the baccalaureate education of most African American scientists and engineers until the 1970s. As recently as 1968, nearly 80 percent of all baccalaureate degrees and almost 50 percent of the graduate degrees awarded to African Americans were granted by HBCUs. Even with the advent of desegregation in higher education, HBCUs have continued to play a prominent role. At the graduate level, the contribution of HBCUs is more recent. Because of severe restrictions during legal segregation, graduate work was limited in the HBCUs and most graduate offerings were in the field of education. Only seven HBCUs offered graduate studies in science fields in 1956, when the *Brown vs. Board of Education* decision ending legal segregation was applied to higher education. In the three decades since, the number of HBCUs offering graduate studies in science and engineering has increased to 25, and their offerings cover every major S/E field.

Recent research and scholarship reaffirms the quality of educational life for African Americans at HBCUs (Fleming, 1984; Allen, Epps, and Haniff, 1991) and further documents the crucial productivity these colleges show in both their efficiency (Thomas, 1984) and their proficiency in many key fields (Trent, 1984; Thomas, 1989), notably, the sciences and technical fields.

Although our focus is on students in HBCUs, we must point out that not all students in HBCUs are African American. These institutions have enrolled students of all racial and ethnic groups. The recipients of degrees from HBCUs reflect this:

1. Of the science/engineering bachelor's degrees awarded by HBCUs in 1989, 85 percent were earned by African American U.S. citizens, 9 percent by students of other racial/ethnic groups, and 6 percent by foreign students.
2. At the master's degree level, 49 percent of science/engineering degrees from HBCUs were awarded to African American U.S. citizens, 26 percent to recipients of other racial/ethnic groups, and 25 percent to foreign students.

While the HBCUs are not exclusive, they do provide a supportive atmosphere for African American students.

It is important to place discussions about the role(s) of HBCUs in American higher education today into context. These institutions have been and continue to be the target of attacks on their academic quality. In fact, some question the very need for their continued existence, particularly the public colleges. Campbell (1969) lists a dozen or more criticisms, including funding inadequacies, quality of facilities, and a challenge to their academic standards. Litigation has shown that many of the challenges and obstacles that HBCUs confront are the result of discriminatory practices that have denied the public HBCUs fair and reasonable support.[1]

In a different vein, research and scholarship in education more often examine the psychological access and comfort that colleges and universities provide to students, especially to those who are "nontraditional" on those campuses. Fleming (1990) reports that the HBCU provides an environment that is motivational and supportive for the African American student. Not only are social relations more amenable, but mentoring and the nurturing of academic aspirations are more accessible. The latter is especially critical in the sciences and related fields, where there is substantial evidence that the process of becoming a scientist relies heavily on mentoring (Blackwell, 1981).

These two issues, the material value of HBCUs in terms of efficiency and proficiency and their social value in terms of their ability to provide a nurturing social and academic environment which facilitates success for a broader range of students, are key features of the present context. Preer (1982) argues that aspects of these issues have long been features of the legal history surrounding the HBCU. The trend through the mid-1980s was to pursue the material improvement of the HBCUs and to endorse their special role in American higher education. The success of HBCUs and their principal clients rests on the continuing shape of responses to them. The research presented here may be useful in informing that response.

The HBCU Contribution at the Baccalaureate Level

The HBCUs were the primary source of baccalaureate education for African American scientists for over one hundred years. In the early part of this century, the private HBCUs offered African American students opportunities to study the classical sciences—biology, chemistry, mathematics—and the public HBCUs primarily offered studies in agriculture, mechanics, industrial sciences, and some engineering, reflecting their land-grant status. However, students on HBCU campuses studying science and engineering were overwhelmingly outnumbered by students preparing to be teachers, reflecting the employment discrimination against African Americans.

With the expansion of employment opportunities for African Americans in the early 1970s, the HBCUs changed their curriculum to prepare their students for expanded career choices. In the decade from 1972 to 1982, the HBCUs multiplied their engineering bachelor's awards by a factor of three and their computer science degrees by a factor of eleven; physical science awards also increased and biological sciences maintained their high profile. By the early 1980s, the distribution of bachelor's degree awards by major field at the HBCUs generally reflected that of other institutions in their region (U.S. Department of Education, 1985). In 1989, one-third of the bachelor's degrees awarded at HBCUs were in science and engineering, the same proportion found in other institutions (figs. 4.1 and 4.2). Like other students, African American students appear to follow market patterns that influence field choice irrespective of the racial heritage of the college in which they are enrolled. Indeed, the pattern of changes in degree distribution for the bachelor's degree earned by African American students in HBCUs in 1977, 1981, and 1989 is very similar to the pattern of their counterparts at white colleges and universities.

While the patterns of change are largely comparable, there are important differences and similarities. In business, for example, African American students at TWCUs show a greater concentration (in terms of the fraction of all African American degree recipients from these institutions) than their African American peers at HBCUs, and the change from 1981 to 1989 is increasing at TWCUs but decreasing at HBCUs. In the S/E fields, however, the pattern of change in HBCUs is the same as the pattern in TWCUs. More than just the patterns, the number of degrees awarded is notable. When we compare figures 4.1 and 4.2, focusing on the biological sciences and mathematics, we can see clearly that HBCUs were nearly as productive as TWCUs, despite their smaller number as a subset of colleges and universities.

The 80 HBCUs which award bachelor's degrees in science and engineering are a small proportion of the total number of institutions in this country which award S/E baccalaureates (1,190), yet they play a prominent role in educating African American scientists and engineers. In 1977 and 1989, HBCUs awarded 33 percent and 30 percent of the S/E degrees earned by African Americans in the United States, respectively.

The contribution of HBCUs to the education of African Americans in 1989, as shown in table 4.1, is especially high in some fields of science. For example, in mathematics, the HBCUs awarded almost half (48 percent) of the bachelor's degrees earned by African Americans in 1989; in the physical sciences, they accounted for 46 percent; in the computer sciences, 43

MAJOR FIELD

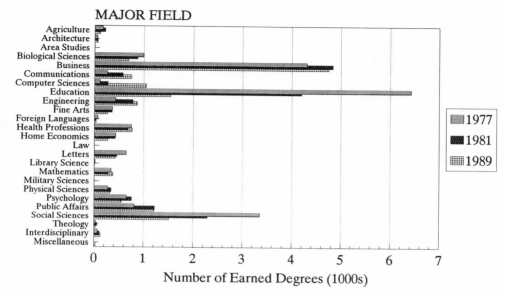

Figure 4.1. Bachelor's degrees earned by African Americans in historically black colleges and universities, 1977, 1981, 1989.

Sources: 1978 and 1981 data are from HEGIS, while 1989 data are from IPEDS. The 1989 detailed major fields have been merged.

percent. In 1989, there were 13 HBCUs that awarded baccalaureates in the field of engineering/engineering technologies. These schools accounted for 28 percent of all such degrees awarded to African Americans.

The fields in which the HBCUs play a relatively smaller role are the social sciences and psychology, where they accounted for 24 and 20 percent, respectively, of all African American bachelor's degree recipients in 1989. It is interesting to note that the HBCUs play a much more prominent role in producing African American natural scientists and engineers than behavioral scientists. This may reflect the greater difficulty that African American students at TWCUs have in persisting in the science and engineering fields compared to their counterparts at HBCUs. As a result, a greater number of African American students at TWCUs may select the social sciences as an alternative.

The persistence in major field explanation leads to the efficiency assessment. We have already noted that HBCUs are overrepresented in degree production among the degree granting schools. Also, a greater proportion of first-time full-time freshmen in HBCUs are degree recipients four to

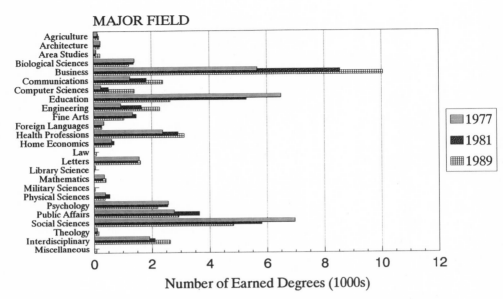

Figure 4.2. Bachelor's degrees earned by African Americans in traditionally white colleges and universities, 1977, 1981, 1989.

Sources: 1977 and 1981 data are from HEGIS, while 1989 data are from IPEDS. The 1989 detailed major fields have been merged.

five years later compared to their counterparts at TWCUs. For example, the ratio of 1981 African American degree recipients from HBCUs to 1976 first-time full-time African American enrollees in HBCUs was 43 percent; the comparable figures for African Americans in TWCUs was 29 percent. While these figures are not cohort estimates and do not correct for transfers, they do suggest a substantial difference in the efficiency of the two institutional contexts in turning new enrollees into degree recipients. This takes on extreme importance when the characteristics of the typical first-time enrollee at an HBCU are compared to their peers at the TWCUs. In the latter institutions, the pool of African American students typically score higher on the admissions exams, have higher class rank, and are generally considered to be better prepared for the college experience than the student pool in HBCUs. The HBCUs enroll a more challenging student population and yet produce a greater proportion of degree recipients from that pool.

Table 4.1. Percentage and Number of African American Bachelor's Degree Recipients in Science and Engineering Fields from Historically Black Colleges and Universities, 1989

| Science/Engineering Field | Number of African Americans in | | % in HBCUs |
	HBCUs*	All Colleges and Universities†	
Total science and engineering	5,498	18,405	30
Engineering/engineering tech.	878	3,154	28
All sciences	4,620	15,251	30
Natural sciences:	2,555	6,171	41
Physical science	320	697	46
Mathematical science	381	792	48
Computer science	1,048	2,467	43
Biological science	693	1,916	36
Agricultural science	113	309	37
Social sciences:	2,065	9,080	23
Social science	1,515	6,337	24
Psychology	550	2,743	20

*In 1989, the total number of historically black colleges and universities (HBCUs) awarding bachelor's degrees in science and engineering was 80.
†In 1989, the total number of colleges and universities awarding bachelor's degrees in science and engineering was 1,110.
Source: U.S. Department of Education, National Center for Education Statistics, IPEDS Completions Survey.

The HBCU Contribution at the Postbaccalaureate Level

Transition to Graduate School

Are African American graduates in science and engineering from HBCUs just as likely to go on to graduate school as those graduates from TWCUs? Data from a national sample survey of recent college graduates in 1987 indicated that approximately 15 percent of African American S/E bachelor's degree recipients from TWCUs went on to graduate school within one year of graduation, a proportion similar to graduates from the HBCUs (U.S. Department of Education, 1987). The comparability of these rates of transition to graduate study are both good and bad news. The good news is that African American graduates of HBCUs are in an environment that develops and sustains their potential for graduate study. The bad news is that African American students at TWCUs, who are on average better students when they exit high school than those African Americans who enroll in HBCUs, are not transitioning to graduate study at a rate commensurate with reasonable expectations. This is especially troublesome because many TWCUs offer a "research mission" environment where aspirations for graduate study are more likely to be nurtured.

Opportunity for Graduate Education for African Americans

Prior to the desegregation of higher education in this country, the African American science and engineering baccalaureates from HBCUs had very few opportunities to continue with graduate studies in their field unless they went outside the South or to Europe. Most of the states which operated dual, segregated public systems of higher education for African Americans and whites did not provide graduate studies in science and engineering for African American residents; many of these states offered "scholarship aid" to their African American residents who wanted to enroll in a graduate program offered by a white university in that state to enable them to attend an out-of-state institution (McCuiston, 1939). These scholarship aid programs had insufficient annual appropriations to meet the demands for graduate education by their African American residents (Federal Security Agency, 1942). This unmet need of the African American community for graduate studies in the sciences and professional fields was a factor that helped to precipitate the legal attacks on the "separate but equal" doctrine in education beginning in the 1930s. As a result of legal cases, a few African American graduate students were admitted, most by court order, to white universities. The *Brown vs. Board of Education* decision of 1954, declaring separate educational facilities inherently unequal, was extended to higher education in 1956 by the U.S. Supreme Court. In that year, there were four private HBCUs (Howard, Fisk, Tuskegee, and Atlanta universities) and three public HBCUs (Tennessee State, Prairie View A&M, and Texas Southern universities) that offered graduate S/E programs (U.S. Department of Health, Education, and Welfare, 1958).

Graduate programs at the HBCUs did not increase generally until the late 1960s. They expanded from 1964 through the mid-1970s in both the number of institutions offering graduate programs and in the size of enrollments (U.S. Department of Education, 1985). By 1989, there were twenty-five HBCUs which offered graduate programs in science and engineering fields. Those twenty-five institutions accounted for one out of five of the total master's degrees in science and engineering awarded to African Americans in 1989, about the same proportion as in 1977. The HBCUs played an especially prominent role in the production of African American recipients of master's degrees in the physical sciences and the biological sciences, in addition to the agricultural sciences. While HBCUs represented just 4 percent of the master's degree–granting colleges and universities, in no S/E field did they award fewer than 11 percent of the master's degrees earned by African Americans (table 4.2).

Table 4.3 presents the results at the doctoral level. At the doctoral degree level, only four HBCUs award S/E degrees: Howard University, Clark

Table 4.2. Percentage and Number of African American Master's Degree Recipients in Science and Engineering Fields from Historically Black Colleges and Universities, 1989

| | Number of African Americans in | | |
S/E Field	HBCU*	All Colleges and Universities†	% in HBCUs
Total science and engineering	326	1,688	19
Engineering/engineering tech.	45	401	11
All sciences	281	1,287	22
Natural sciences	148	512	29
Physical science	23	78	29
Mathematical science	13	59	22
Computer science	42	198	21
Biological sciences	47	124	38
Agricultural science	23	53	43
Social sciences	133	775	17
Social science	78	380	21
Psychology	55	395	14

*In 1989, the number of historically black colleges and universities (HBCUs) awarding master's degrees in science and engineering was 25.
†In 1989, the total number of universities awarding master's degrees in science and engineering was 615.
Source: U.S. Department of Education, National Center for Education Statistics, IPEDS Completions Survey.

Atlanta University, Meharry Medical College, and the University of Maryland at Eastern Shore. These four universities conferred a total of eighty-four degrees to African Americans over a five-year period from 1985 to 1989, accounting for only 2 percent of African American S/E doctorate recipients nationally.

However, when the baccalaureate origins of African American doctorates are examined, the contribution of the HBCUs is significant. Among African American doctorates in S/E fields from 1976 to 1978, 43 percent had attended an HBCU for their undergraduate degree, continuing a tradition of producing African American scientific talent (Pearson and Pearson, 1985). However, among doctorates earned in 1986–88, HBCUs provided the undergraduate education of 29 percent of recent African American doctorates in S/E fields overall. They accounted for 36 percent of the baccalaureate origins of African American Ph.D.'s in engineering, 26 percent in the natural sciences, and 24 percent of those in the social sciences.

The contribution of HBCUs to the graduate training of African Americans is clearly demonstrated in these data. Indeed, the contribution is both direct and indirect. On the one hand, the few graduate programs that exist in HBCUs contribute far more than a reasonably expected share to the

Table 4.3. Overview of the Role of Historically Black Colleges and Universities
(HBCUs) among African Americans in Conferral of Science
and Engineering Degrees, by Level, 1989

Number of HBCUs*	Level of S/E Degree	Degrees from HBCUs*	HBCUs as a Percentage of all Degrees
80	Bachelor's degrees	5,498	30
25	Master's degrees	326	19
4	Doctorate degrees	84†	2
80	Baccalaureate origins of doctorates	691‡	29

Note: Data are for black U.S. citizens or holders of permanent visas. S/E, science and engineering.
* Excludes foreign citizens on permanent resident visas.
†Doctorates from 1985–89.
‡Doctorates from 1985–88.
Source: U.S. Department of Education, National Center for Education Statistics, IPEDS Completions
Survey, and Survey of Earned Doctorates.

supply of African American recipients of the master's and doctorate degrees. In addition, the HBCUs also provide a substantial share of the pool
of eligible graduates in S/E who subsequently undertake graduate study
at TWCUs.

Conclusions

HBCUs have served as the conduit for the education of African American students in science and engineering for over one hundred years, and
even with the advent of desegregation in this country, they continue to
play a prominent role in the production of African American scientists and
engineers. They take students who may not have been well prepared in
high school for careers in the "hard sciences" and graduate them with
degrees in S/E. TWCUs are more likely to graduate African American
students in the social sciences, even though their students may have, on
the average, better preparation in high school than those who attend
HBCUs. In effect, HBCUs appear to better fit the popular characterization
of education as a meritocratic process by which schools serve the vital
function of identifying and developing talent wherever it resides, irrespective of the student's ascriptive characteristics.

The impact of the role played by HBCUs among African Americans in
S/E education is greatest at the baccalaureate level, both in terms of the
number of degrees awarded and in the number of their baccalaureate recipients who go on to earn a doctorate degree in science and engineering.
HBCUs contribute almost one-third of the pool of African American baccalaureates in S/E. Of these graduates, 15 percent go on to graduate school,

as do African American graduates of TWCUs. This is reflected in the fact that three out of ten of the recent African American doctorate recipients earned their baccalaureate at an HBCU. At the master's degree level, the few HBCUs (25) which offer graduate programs produce one out of five of all the African American master's degree recipients in this country.

HBCUs contribute more to the pool of African American natural scientists and engineers than to the pool of social and behavioral scientists. While the HBCUs account for around one out of five African American baccalaureates in the social sciences, their contribution in the natural sciences is almost twice as high. The proportion of this nation's African American degree recipients who are educated in the HBCUs is very high in the natural sciences—around four out of ten recipients at the baccalaureate level and three out of ten at the master's degree level. Engineering and engineering technology programs have grown considerably in the HBCUs. As a result, these institutions now account for 30 percent of African American bachelor's and almost 20 percent of African American master's degree recipients in engineering and engineering technologies.

The results reported here demonstrate that HBCUs serve as a vital national resource in the production of African American scientists and engineers, especially at the baccalaureate level. The HBCUs have not historically had the resources and support to build the foundations of graduate research programs, and while their role is important in this area, the number of African American graduates produced by HBCUs has declined in recent years. If this national resource is to be used to alleviate the decline in African Americans participating in the sciences (Matthew, 1990), a concerted effort must be made to increase the resources available to these institutions. Such an effort would involve federal, state, and private sector scientific organizations that support science and engineering education and research (Institute for Science, Space, and Technology, 1990). These resources must be sufficient to enhance student support—tuition and expenses at the undergraduate and graduate level—as well as institutional support. Institutional support has to fund the involvement of faculty and students in research and the development of the infrastructure in ways that sustain quality preparation in science and engineering.

It appears that in those fields where resources and market needs have stimulated growth, both HBCUs and their students have responded. This suggests that resources and support, rather than competencies and tradition, are major factors constraining the contribution of HBCUs, especially in the science and science-related fields. The enhancement strategies for HBCUs articulated during the *Adams* era remain viable, if not essential. Central among these is the need to improve and expand instructional resources and faculty research support. In a period of fiscal stringency that

limits government action—including investment in education—the increasing need for a more highly skilled labor supply provides a strong case
for strengthening the role of one of the more efficient and productive
sources of African American degree holders. Failure to do so not only
threatens those institutions and their traditional clients, it also threatens
the supply of a substantial talent pool for the work force and for graduate
training.

Note

1. *Adams vs. Richardson* (356 F. Supp. 92. D.C. 1973). With the plaintiffs in
Adams having been declared without standing, it is again the role of the states to
rectify the historical disparities.

Chapter 5

Bachelor's Degree Chemists, 1970–1990:
Past Choices and Future Prospects

Terrence Russell

The men and women who hold a bachelor's degree in chemistry as their highest academic degree are an important resource for chemistry and science generally. "B.S. chemists" (for convenience, the term references holders of both B.S. and B.A. degrees) are the pool of U.S. residents from which future chemistry Ph.D.'s (80 percent of them) and M.D.'s (9 percent of the 1990 medical school class) (NRC, 1990; AAMC, 1990) are recruited and the basic pool of scientific and technical manpower for chemical and related industries. As a result of the utility of their education, B.S. chemists are the most heterogeneous of all chemist groups and the most mobile: even at graduation, two-thirds of them intend to be something else—a Ph.D., an M.D., an M.B.A.—in the near future. The mobility of many B.S. chemists is more than a change in credentials. The migration out of chemistry to other careers, and hence the diffusion of chemical knowledge throughout the occupational spectrum, is primarily an outflow of B.S. holders utilizing their scientific training in other fields.

In this chapter I describe the past and present circumstances of B.S. chemists and, based on this description, make some forecasts about these people and those who will be the graduates of four-year chemistry programs in the 1990s. A number of private and federal agencies collect data on chemists, but to chart the situation of the B.S. graduate, I draw on data sets maintained by the National Science Foundation and the National Research Council, on both B.S. and, for comparison, Ph.D. holders. For clarity, this analysis will not deal with the situation of M.S. chemists, who, on most indicators, fall between the B.S. and Ph.D. groups, as intuition would tell us. I also draw heavily on our own ACS Comprehensive Member Surveys and the Starting Salary Surveys of new graduates so identified by their academic departments. To simplify comparisons, I used the ACS data sets for 1975, 1980, 1985, and 1989 (the latest available data set). Within and across these selected years, analysis was based on the following "professional age groups": 1 or less, 5–9, 15–19, and 30–35 years since the B.S. was granted. These groups were selected to represent entry, early, mid-, and late career chemists.

General Demographics: The B.S. Chemist and the Educational Pipeline

The negative impact on science of changes in the past and future annual number of 22-year-olds in the U.S. population has received considerable discussion in the science work force literature and needs little comment here except to note that the decline in these cohorts of possible "traditional" B.S. graduates continues until 1997. While other factors may influence the number of B.S. graduates in the 1990s, growth in the available pool of U.S. nationals is not going to make more recruits available for undergraduate education generally or in chemistry. Competition for college-age men and women from industry and the military will also decrease the available college-going pool and the "nontraditional" (over age 22, predominately female) students that increased enrollments in the 1980s will not be a factor in the 1990s, especially for the physical sciences and other quantitative disciplines. As Bowen and Sosa (1989) noted, after the surge in college going by women in the 1980s, there is no comparable pool of women lacking college degrees in the 1990s. Further, the quantitative science disciplines did not receive their share of the 1980s nontraditional students because of their mathematics demands and it is not likely that the situation will be different in the 1990s.

If we look at the past, the probable effect of this general trend on the number of chemistry graduates is clear and not heartening. Figure 5.1 shows the fraction of all bachelor's degrees accounted for by chemistry degrees; a steadily declining fraction from 1979 onward and, from 1970 to 1988, a 37 percent decline in chemistry's "market share" of new B.S./B.A. graduates. Even worse, while the absolute number of B.S./B.A. degrees granted annually increased 25 percent between 1970 (792,656) and 1988 (989,000), the annual number of chemistry B.S. degrees granted fell 22 percent during the same period (11,519 to 9,025). Between the intervening peak year of 1979 (11,509 chemistry B.S. degrees) and 1988, the number of chemistry degrees awarded declined an average of 2.4 percent per year, this during an overall *increase* in B.S./B.A. degrees awarded. Preliminary data indicate that we may expect an accelerating decline for 1989 and 1990 with the general demographic situation adding to the historic trend of 2.4 percent annual loss. It is possible that as few as 8,000 B.S. degrees in chemistry were awarded in 1990.[1]

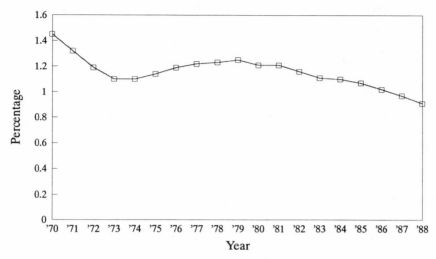

Figure 5.1. Chemistry degrees as a proportion of all bachelor's degrees, 1970–1988.

These declines are not uniform across all types of students. In particular, the number of B.S. chemistry degrees awarded to women increased spectacularly between 1970 and 1988: 74 percent in absolute number, 122 percent as a proportion of all chemistry B.S. degrees. In 1988, 3,586 women accounted for about 40 percent of the B.S. chemistry degrees awarded. Unfortunately, figure 5.2 shows that this increase in women's participation, occurring as it does during an overall decline, masks the fact that the increase in the proportion of women among B.S. graduates is due as much to the decreasing participation of men as to the increase by women. The 5,439 men taking B.S. degrees in chemistry in 1988 was a decline of 42 percent from the 1970 total of 9,453.

The ACS starting salary surveys (table 5.1) show 1975–89 trends in the number of minority B.S. chemistry graduates (earlier data are not available in this series). Most notable is the increase in the percentage of Asians, from 2.4 percent in 1975 to 7.0 percent in 1989. Participation of blacks rose from 1.6 percent in 1975 to a peak of 3.0 percent in 1983, declined again to 1.5 percent in 1987 and by 1989 had returned to 3.0 percent. Because of the small numbers of graduates involved, a good deal of this fluctuation may be response variability across the years, but we can safely say that this is a small group of chemists, both in absolute numbers and as a proportion of the total. The same kind of fluctuation is seen in the similar proportions of Hispanic students, which ranged from 0.3 percent to 2.7 percent over the same period. Because these groups are small, national data beyond the start-

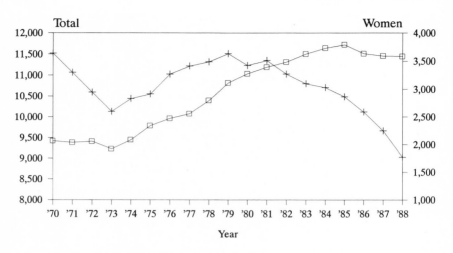

⊟ B.S. chemistry degrees to women   + Total B.S. chemistry degrees

Figure 5.2. Bachelor's degrees awarded in chemistry, 1970–1988.

ing salary data are not available specifically for chemistry B.S. graduates. For the same reason, the ACS sample survey data that are available will not allow us to make a more detailed analysis of these groups.

The question of the generality of this decline in B.S. chemistry degrees can be answered by comparing the "market share" of B.S. chemistry degrees granted by various types of institutions across time. Figure 5.3 compares institutions grouped by the Carnegie Foundation classifications.[2] The striking thing about this graph is the stability of market shares, with some minimal shifts. The 1980s saw an increased percentage of degrees granted by the comprehensive-1 and comprehensive-2 institutions and decreases in all other categories, testimony to the success of these institutions in bringing higher education to a large and diverse public, the increased costs of higher education in other types of institutions, and a cultural image of chemistry as a mobility-driven occupational choice attractive to the middle- and lower-middle-class students who were in the majority at these institutions in the 1970s and 1980s. The largest decline across the 19-year period studied was in the liberal arts-2 percentage share, which dropped from 9 percent in 1970 to a bit more than 5 percent in 1989. As with the comprehensive institutions, this is a general trend in market share that is not unique to chemistry or science majors.

Because of their special role in promoting participation in science by African Americans, trends in the predominately black institutions merit

Table 5.1. Bachelor's Degree Recipients in Chemistry by Race/Ethnicity (%),
1975–1989

Year	American Indian	Asian	Black*	Hispanic	White/Other/ NR†
1975	.1	2.4	1.6	1.0	94.9
1976	.2	1.7	1.9	1.3	94.9
1977	.3	2.9	1.8	1.7	93.2
1978	.1	3.1	1.8	1.0	93.9
1979	.3	2.8	2.0	1.4	93.4
1980	.3	3.6	2.3	1.7	92.2
1981	.4	3.7	3.1	1.9	90.8
1982	.2	4.2	2.6	2.2	90.9
1983	.2	3.3	3.0	2.7	90.9
1984	1.8	5.2	2.1	.3	90.7
1985	.2	4.4	2.8	1.9	90.7
1986	.5	3.8	2.4	2.4	90.9
1987	.1	5.4	1.5	1.6	91.4
1988	.4	7.3	2.3	1.9	88.1
1989	.5	7.0	3.0	2.2	87.3

*Includes African Americans and foreign blacks.
†NR, ethnicity not reported.
Source: ACS Starting Salaries of Chemists and Chemical Engineers, 1975–1989 (individual reports).

close attention. Figure 5.4 shows the total B.S. chemistry degrees granted by 104 such institutions between 1970 and 1989. To those who expect that minority involvement in chemistry will help offset losses in the total number of B.S. chemists, figure 5.4 is not good news. If one compares figure 5.4 with figure 5.2, it is obvious that the experience of the predominately black institutions is little different from others; the decline in chemistry degrees granted during the 1980s closely tracks the overall decline. If one looks at the experience of specific institutions across the 1970–89 time period, the concentration of B.S. chemistry graduates in just a few institutions (most with some reputation for premedical education) is clear. The five highest-producing institutions (4.8 percent of the 104) granted 38 percent of the 357 B.S. chemistry degrees in 1970 and 36 percent of 277 in 1989. However, there has been considerable change among these 104 institutions across the years. Only Howard University was among the five highest producers in both 1970 and 1989, and it was the only institution to be there consistently across the time period studied. For comparison, of the 593 chemistry departments reporting their 1989 degree production to the ACS Committee on Professional Training, the top-producing 4.8 percent (28 departments) accounted for only 20 percent of the total. By themselves, the University of Illinois and Indiana University granted 250 B.S. chemistry degrees, 90 percent of the production of all the predominately

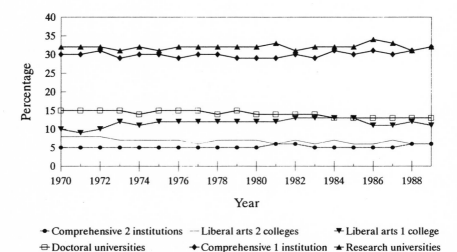

Figure 5.3. Annual percentage shares of bachelor's degrees in chemistry, 1970–1988.

Source: Department of Education.

black institutions (ACS-CPT, 1990). These comparisons highlight the difficulty of constructing stable "feeder" relationships between chemistry programs in the predominately black institutions and graduate programs in the large research institutions. Assuming that the more general pattern among B.S. graduates holds for graduates of the predominately black institutions (approximately equal thirds of the class to graduate school, medical school, and to work; see the discussion below), there were, among these 104 schools, about 90 graduate school–bound B.S. holders in the class of 1989. If they were distributed as chemistry graduates generally, 34 came from the five top-producing schools, leaving 56 graduates distributed among the other 99. As for the five top producers, Xavier University–New Orleans was the largest in 1989 and well known as a producer of medical students. Howard University (the second largest that year) also is an important feeder school for medical schools (including its own) and, as well, has its own chemistry Ph.D. program to recruit for. In this sparse situation, it is difficult for undergraduate departments to maintain long-standing ties to graduate institutions that would allow for the development of firm graduate school expectations among future students.

To get at the implications of these trends for the educational and labor markets that depend on the supply of B.S. chemists, one has to understand

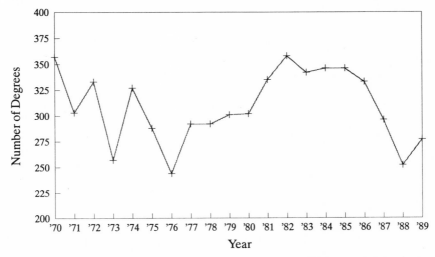

Figure 5.4. Bachelor's degrees in chemistry awarded by 104 predominantly black institutions, 1970–1989.

the patterns of choice that the B.S. chemist makes at various career points: to continue education in chemistry or another field, to work at the bench, or to work in marketing or in management.

The most basic career choice a new B.S. chemist makes is whether to continue on to graduate school. Because chemistry Ph.D. programs recruit very few new students without a chemistry B.S. (20 percent or less), the number of U.S. students recruited to these programs varies with the available annual supply of chemistry B.S. graduates; open places for students must then be filled by immigration. To get some idea of the impact of the pattern of choice and persistence of B.S. chemists entering Ph.D. programs, we began with the number of Ph.D.'s awarded to U.S. residents in 1970 and divided it by the number of 1964 B.S. chemistry graduates, taking six years as an estimate of the length of time necessary to complete the Ph.D. The same fraction was calculated for each Ph.D. class through 1989. The results were somewhat surprising: the "Ph.D. yield" of those B.S. classes from 1964 to 1983 was almost a constant, ranging between 12 and 13 percent. Given declines in the size of the B.S. classes, the modest annual increases in the numbers of Ph.D.'s granted in the 1980s are due solely to the increased participation of foreign students.

Not every B.S. chemist pursues further education, and those who do, do not necessarily pursue full-time studies in chemistry. The 1989 ACS

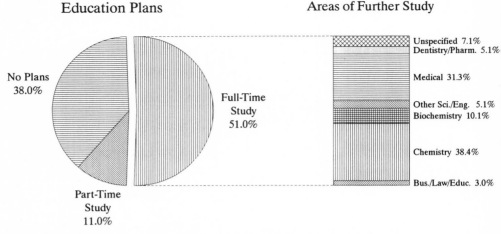

Figure 5.5. Further education plans of graduates with B.S. degrees, 1989.

Source: 1989 ACS Starting Salary Survey.

Starting Salary Survey shows the contemporary pattern of education choices for new B.S. graduates. In this study, which asked about the further education plans of B.S. chemists, 38 percent had no plans, 51 percent planned full-time study, and 11 percent planned part-time study. There were no differences between holders of ACS certified and noncertified degrees and some differences between men and women who planned full-time study (54 percent and 47 percent, respectively) and no further study (women: 43 percent; men: 36 percent). Unfortunately, we have no data on past graduates that would indicate the extent to which these new graduates may return to further education after stopping out for a period, nor useful data to make estimates for minorities in chemistry.

Figure 5.5 shows the curriculum choices of the 51 percent of the 1989 B.S. class who planned full-time study immediately following graduation. Not surprisingly, chemistry leads the list: 38 percent of those planning full-time study will do so in chemistry. More surprising is the nearly equal percentage (31 percent) who plan to go to medical school. A survey-based estimate of 1,400 chemistry-trained medical students in the 1989–90 class compares well with the actual 1,480 B.S. chemists reported by the AAMC (1990) as accepted into medical schools. Given reports of the increase in interest in careers in business among contemporary students, the other interesting finding is the low number of new graduates intending to pursue an M.B.A. or law degree: less than 3 percent of the full-time students.

B.S. Chemists in the Work Force, 1975–1989

While many new B.S. graduates go on to further education, a large number, usually about one-third of each graduating class, do not. Let us consider the career characteristics of those chemists who enter the work force with a bachelor's degree and compare their experiences across the period 1975–89. The primary source for this analysis is the ACS comprehensive member survey series (ACS, 1975a, 1980a, 1985a, 1989a). Where necessary in analyzing the experiences of new entrants, we have also used data from the ACS starting salary survey series (ACS, 1975b, 1980b, 1985b, 1989b). While there may be some differences between B.S. chemists who are ACS members and those who are not, this data set is the only one available that provides the necessary detailed information on B.S. chemists. Further, comparisons with NSF and Bureau of Labor Statistics data sets show no important differences on those characteristics for which comparable data exist.

We have selected data for four years across the 1975–89 span: 1975, 1980, 1985, and 1989. Within each of those years and based on the time since the B.S. degree was granted, we selected four groups of B.S. chemists to represent chemists at four career stages: new entrants (less than 1 year since the B.S.), early career (5–9 years since the B.S.), mid-career (15–19 years since the B.S.), and late career (30–35 years since the B.S.). The percentage of B.S. chemists found in these four ACS survey samples varied little over the fifteen-year period. In 1975, they were 28 percent of the sample; in 1980, 26 percent; in 1985, 32 percent; and in 1989, 24 percent. This small variation reflects the stability in the size of the B.S. chemist group in the work force as well as in the ACS membership.

The other prominent characteristic of B.S. chemists that has remained stable over time is their relative salary level, although absolute salaries have kept pace with inflation. When we compare the salaries of B.S. chemists to that of Ph.D.'s, as shown in figure 5.6, one can see that, with the exception of the midcareer group (15–19 years) in 1980, there is almost no change across the years at all professional career stages. For a fifteen-year period, new B.S. entrants into the work force earned approximately 60 percent of the earnings of their Ph.D. colleagues and, at later career stages, 75–80 percent. While there is more than salary involved in assessing the status of educational credentials in occupational fields, salary is important. In salary terms, the status of B.S. chemists has not changed in relation to Ph.D.'s.

Other characteristics of B.S. chemists have changed over fifteen years, however, and give us some clues for the future of this group. Most basic

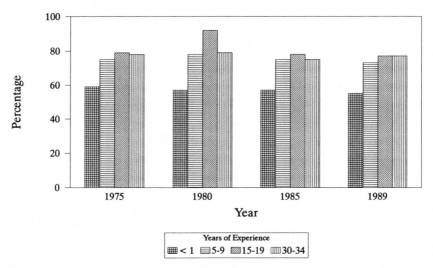

Figure 5.6. Salaries of chemists with B.S. degrees as a percentage of salaries of chemists with Ph.D.'s, 1975–1989.

are demographic shifts. Figure 5.7 shows the relative size of professional age groups in each of the four years sampled. The most dramatic change in the profiles is the growth of the proportion of B.S. chemists in the 5–9 year category, from 13 percent in 1975 to 21 percent in 1989. Part of this increase is purely demographic, as the peak of 22 percent in 1985 indicates. Historically, over 95 percent of all B.S. graduates have received the degree by age 22: the 1985 5–9 year class are the baby boomers. Demography is not everything, however. The proportion of B.S. chemists who are new entrants has remained fairly stable, while the fifteen-year decrease from 11 percent to 6 percent in the oldest professional age group studied (roughly the 52- to 56-year-old group) is testimony to professional attrition among older B.S. chemists.

In career terms, we are faced with an age distribution that has large numbers of people who will be looking forward to upward mobility in, for the most part, large organizations with fewer positions available for promotion than people qualified to get promoted. Especially in the chemical industry, it is not clear how well these soon-to-be-midcareer B.S. chemists will be able to compete with their colleagues with advanced degrees for managerial positions at the mid-level and above. This kind of age distribution is, however, typical for a work force resource pool, which is still young enough to provide "outflows" to higher education and other occupations which could utilize their skills.

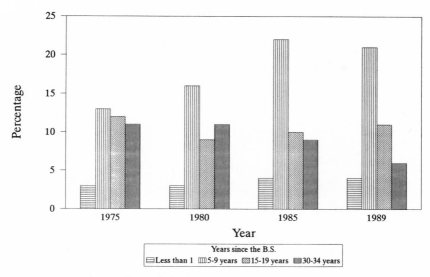

Figure 5.7. Professional age shifts, 1975–1989.

Changes in the employment of B.S. chemists, particularly the work specialties of choice, are a strong indication that these are service sector workers, not manufacturing workers. The period 1975–89 saw the rapid growth of analytical chemistry as the specialty of choice, especially for new entrants. This was true regardless of the distribution of employment by sector. Figure 5.8 shows that in 1975, 33 percent of the new entrants indicated analytical chemistry as their work specialty. By 1989, 46 percent called themselves analytical chemists and, in addition, 17 percent listed themselves as environmental chemists, a category not available in the 1975 survey and a specialty whose content at the B.S. level is largely analytical chemistry.

In addition to these trends in work specialty choices that operate across the years, there is also a dual track across work functions as B.S. chemists move through their careers. A look at figure 5.9 shows that the career progression is to begin in a research job or marketing and, as a senior employee, go on to a management position. In all sampled years, the proportion of people in research shrinks, the proportion of those in marketing stays stable, and the proportion of managers increases. This is a career pattern that uses the B.S. degree and research work as an entry to management rather than as a career in itself based on accumulating technical and scientific expertise.

There is some evidence of an emerging career pattern that may have

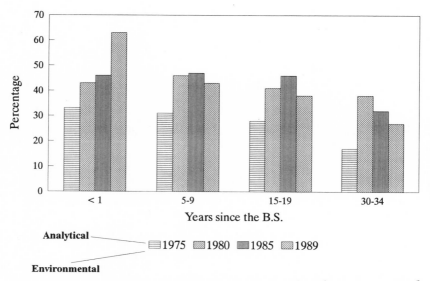

Figure 5.8. Chemists with B.S. degrees working in analytical or environmental chemistry.

different career implications, especially in terms of movement into management. Historically, the "premanagerial" B.S. research worker began a career, at least formally, as a professional employee, not as a support worker. Research support technicians with the B.S. are beginning to be more common as industry new hires in professional research positions increasingly are restricted to those with advanced degrees. In both the 1988 and 1989 starting salary survey samples, 38 percent of the new B.S. degree holders taking employment took positions titled "technician." While some individual technicians have been able to follow the research-to-management career path, it would seem that the mobility chances of a B.S. chemist in this position would be diminished, especially as advancement in research positions increasingly requires an advanced degree. The net effect of this development may be an increasing demand for continuing chemistry education as technicians attempt to advance within research careers.

The Future of the B.S. Degree Holder in Chemistry

Forecasting work force futures is always a tricky business, but I think the forecast for the 1990s that follows is highly probable, given what has been shown here about B.S. chemists. I have already discussed the effects

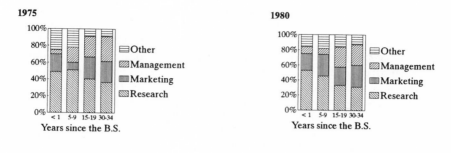

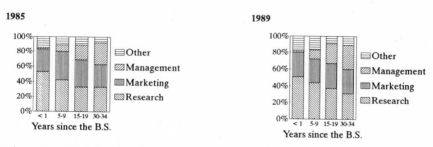

Figure 5.9. Work function by years since receiving the B.S. degree, 1975–1989.

of the U.S. demographic decline on college going in the 1990s (and hence on the number of B.S. chemists), but what is left to discuss is the impact on science and industry of a reduced number of U.S. residents with B.S. degrees and how the demographic decline will affect life choices that will in turn affect the career decisions of B.S. chemists. Because of the clear trend toward increase in women's participation, the impact of women's work and family choices is quite central. Historical demographers tell us that generally, in good economic times, family size increases. While I do not propose to forecast the condition of the economy over the next ten years, the smaller cohorts entering the labor force in the 1990s will mean less competition and presumably higher wages and a labor market favoring the employee: good times indeed to those who entered the labor market in the late 1970s and early 1980s, whatever the larger economic situation (short of collapse). "Increased family size" has also meant that, histori-cally, women left the labor force for child care, leaving jobs that were held primarily out of economic necessity. Their leaving further reduced the labor pool, with the happy consequence of improving the labor market (from the employee's point of view) and presumably increasing wages as well. So much for the past. The question for the 1990s is whether women

B.S. chemists will have larger families and decreasing work force participation, just larger families, or neither. It appears that as a highly educated professional group, "neither" is the best forecast for women chemists. At this juncture, we also do not know if women will continue to be recruited to chemistry in the same proportion as in the 1980s. Indeed, the absolute number of women taking B.S. degrees in chemistry began to decline in 1986. The effect of that recruiting pattern on the age distribution on the 1990s will be to maintain the domination of the baby boomers, a group that will likely have completed their childbearing before the 1990s are far along.

In addition to family choices, educational and occupational choices in this kind of a labor market will not favor graduate education, at least not as a first option for those taking one of the most salable of the liberal arts and sciences degrees. Graduate education will increasingly be deferred, and in a really good job market, higher salaries will make it harder to return to school, especially for those students who chose to take a chemistry degree precisely because it provides ready entry into the technical employment market. The value choice of job over graduate school is, it seems to me, an inheritance of the occupational structure of the 1980s, and it is possible that a "good times" labor market may make graduate school appear somewhat safer as an occupational alternative. In the end, however, I think there is little hope for a large-scale reversal of the declining numbers of U.S. chemistry students interested in graduate school during the 1990s. Whatever industry's need for participation by foreign nationals in the next ten years, U.S. graduate programs will not be able to operate without them.

Industrial demand for B.S. chemists in the 1990s will depend on both market conditions and organizational changes in industry and changes in the technology. This occurs not only in production sectors of the economy but in government and service (particularly medical and health care) sectors as well. Driven by increasing consumer sophistication, higher levels of demand for more diverse products and the wide utility of chemistry education for nonchemical areas of industry (computing, marketing, etc.), these demand factors for B.S. chemists will operate primarily at the entry level and will serve to increase the heterogeneity of the B.S. chemist work force.

The increasing complexity and sophistication of chemical and related technology will continue to force upgrades in the sophistication of technician work and increase the educational requirements for entry-level science jobs. In the 1990s, the B.S. degree will become the basic requirement for entry into technical industrial jobs, making the declining numbers of B.S. graduates an even greater problem unless we find ways to bring the required technical skill and training to the workplace in other ways. If we cannot attract more students to the study of chemistry, the skill requirements of industry must be met through the codification of skill in computer-assisted equipment, through technical training that lacks the breadth of a B.S. degree, or through utilization of the skills of immigrants. If we do not find a way to bring the necessary skill and training to the workplace, most assuredly the workplace will go to those places where the skill of the B.S. chemist does exist.

Notes

1. As this chapter was going to press, NSF data became available indicating that the overall trend in B.S. chemistry degrees reversed between 1990 and 1991: 1989, 8,654 degrees awarded; 1990, 8,132; 1991, 8,321. The percentage of women receiving B.S. chemistry degrees remained fairly stable for the period 1988–91: 1988, 39.7 percent; 1989, 38.6 percent, 1990, 39.8 percent; 1991, 40.1 percent, ending a string of annual percentage increases beginning in 1968.

2. The Carnegie Foundation developed the following classifications used in figure 5.3.

Research universities: Offer a full range of B.A./B.S. programs, and doctorate degrees. They receive annually at least $12.5 million in federal support and award at least 50 Ph.D. degrees each year.

Doctoral-granting universities: Offer a full range of B.A./B.S. programs and doctorate degrees. They award at least 20 Ph.D. degrees annually in at least one discipline or 10 or more Ph.D. degrees in three or more disciplines.

Comprehensive universities and colleges 1: Offer B.A./B.S. programs and the master's degree. More than half of their B.A./B.S. degrees are awarded in two or more occupational or professional disciplines. Enroll at least 2,500 students.

Comprehensive universities and colleges 2: Award more than half of their B.A./B.S. degrees in two or more occupational or professional disciplines and many offer the master's degree. Enroll between 1,500 and 2,500 students.

Liberal arts colleges 1: Highly selective institutions are primarily undergraduate colleges that award more than half of their baccalaureate degrees in arts and science fields.

Liberal arts colleges 2: Less selective colleges that award more than half of their degrees in liberal arts fields. Also includes colleges that award less than half of their degrees in liberal arts fields and enroll fewer than 1,500 students.

CHAPTER 6

Trends in Science and Engineering Doctorate Production, 1975–1990

Earl Smith and Joyce Tang

As the United States shifts from manufacturing to service-oriented industries, the demand for workers with specialized knowledge and skills will undoubtedly increase (Reich, 1991; NSB, 1990). At the international level, the competition for scarce resources and a commanding place on the world market are all indications of the need to seriously examine issues related to the production of doctorates in America. The present and future of U.S. industries, worldwide, will depend on the nation's ability to attract and develop human capital. And, while there is little disagreement between the public and private sectors that a large number of Americans who graduate from our universities with advanced degrees in science and engineering will boost our economy, there is considerable disagreement about how to make the increases in higher education in science and engineering actually happen.

By many standards, despite the country's strong commitment to research and development (R&D), our economic and industrial competitiveness in the global economy is declining (Dertouzos et al., 1989; Marglin and Schor, 1989; Porter, 1989). One of the major concerns in the private sector is the production of more sophisticated and highly skilled workers. Many agree that to better position themselves both at home and abroad in the coming decades, U.S. companies need to hire more skilled scientists and engineers (Bernstein, 1988; Coates, Jarrat, and Mahaffie, 1990). It is ironic that some scholars are also predicting that the United States will have a shortage of some thousands of Ph.D.–trained scientists and engineers by the end of this century, largely due to demographic changes and attrition (Atkinson, 1990; Brown and Clewell, 1991; Holden, 1989).[1]

Thus, one of the major issues facing the nation today is how capable its human capital stock is of meeting the challenges of tomorrow. Specifically, what kind of work force will lead us into the next century? To answer this question, we need to know several things: we need to update our knowledge of the most educated strata of the scientific and engineering work force—the doctorate scientists and engineers. Furthermore, we need to follow their trends, origin, field of training, and patterns of utilization in the U.S. economy.

In this chapter we examine trends in the number of doctoral degrees conferred to U.S. citizens in science and engineering fields from 1975 to 1990. We provide a detailed background of the Ph.D. populations by demographic character, career prospects, employment patterns, academic rank, and economic status. The chapter begins with an overview of minority and female representation in the science and engineering doctoral population, followed by discussion of their field of training, parents' educational background, sources of financial support, duration of degree completion, and postgraduation career plans. In the second part of the chapter we examine the career prospects of minority and female Ph.D.'s, focusing on their rates and sector of employment, the status of academic doctorates, as well as their earnings levels in both the public and private sectors.

The profile draws on cross-sectional and trend data—the Survey of Earned Doctorates (SED) and the Survey of Doctorate Recipients (SDR).[2] It highlights the differences and similarities among whites, African Americans, Asians, Hispanics,[3] and Native Americans,[4] as well as between males and females, in mathematics, computer sciences, engineering, and the physical, life, social, and behavioral sciences.[5] Unfortunately, the data do not allow us to make subgroup comparisons among Asians and Hispanics. Our focus is on native and foreign-born science and engineering (S/E) doctorates with U.S. citizenship.[6]

Demographic Portrait of the Science and Engineering Ph.D. Population

Most of the Ph.D.'s awarded to U.S. citizens go to white, non-Hispanics (NRC, 1991b).[7] For the sixteen-year period from 1975 to 1990, the production of Ph.D.'s in the United States has been constant. After the initial decline that took place between 1976 and 1978, the largest number of Ph.D.'s produced held steady until 1985. However, these data obscure the fact that the number of S/E doctorates granted to women, African Americans, Hispanics, and Native Americans has more than doubled. It is these increases that we now examine.

Table 6.1 reports the overall and field distribution of doctoral degrees awarded to U.S. citizens by gender and race or ethnicity between 1975 and 1990. The number of S/E doctoral degrees granted to U.S. citizens has increased by only 1 percent in sixteen years, from a total of 14,475 in 1975 to 14,627 in 1990. The good news, though, is that the number of minori-

Table 6.1. Doctorates in Science and Engineering Awarded to U.S. Citizens, by Gender, Race/Ethnicity, and Field, 1975–1990

Year and Field	Men	Women	Total*	Native Americans	Asians	African Americans	Hispanics	Whites
1975 (all fields)	11,942	2,533	14,475	14	201	261	137	13,240
Index of Dissimilarity (D)†		(30)		(33)	(18)	(23)	(6)	
Physical sciences	22%	8%	19%	0%	19%	12%	14%	19%
MCSE‡	20%	5%	18%	29%	36%	8%	17%	18%
Life sciences	26%	33%	27%	14%	27%	21%	28%	28%
Psychology	15%	32%	18%	36%	6%	29%	22%	18%
Social sciences	17%	22%	18%	21%	11%	30%	19%	18%
1980 (all fields)	10,259	3,476	13,735	28	329	281	174	12,143
Index of Dissimilarity (D)		(25)		(12)	(16)	(21)	(14)	
Physical sciences	21%	8%	17%	18%	19%	5%	13%	17%
MCSE‡	17%	4%	14%	11%	26%	8%	13%	14%
Life sciences	31%	34%	32%	11%	26%	8%	13%	14%
Psychology	16%	35%	21%	25%	31%	23%	21%	33%
Social sciences	15%	18%	16%	25%	12%	23%	24%	15%
1985 (all fields)	9,127	4,246	13,373	42	380	293	254	12,048
Index of Dissimilarity (D)		(26)		(20)	(18)	(25)	(14)	
Physical sciences	23%	10%	19%	10%	22%	9%	12%	19%
MCSE†	18%	5%	14%	2%	28%	8%	11%	13%
Life sciences	32%	36%	33%	45%	34%	24%	30%	34%
Psychology	15%	33%	21%	24%	9%	34%	25%	21%
Social sciences	12%	16%	13%	19%	7%	25%	22%	13%
1990 (all fields)	9,358	5,269	14,627	41	508	308	396	13,111
Index of Dissimilarity (D)		(29)		(25)	(17)	(27)	(11)	
Physical sciences	23%	10%	18%	10%	18%	7%	19%	19%
MCSE‡	24%	8%	18%	12%	35%	11%	13%	18%
Life sciences	29%	36%	32%	22%	30%	24%	26%	32%
Psychology	13%	33%	20%	44%	9%	36%	25%	20%
Social sciences	11%	13%	12%	12%	8%	22%	18%	12%

Note: Degrees in humanities, education, and professional fields are excluded.

* Includes doctorates with unknown race/ethnicity categories.

† Percentage of women (or minorities) who would have to change fields of specialization to be distributed in the same manner as men (or whites).

‡ Mathematics, computer sciences, and engineering.

Sources: The Survey of Earned Doctorates and the Survey of Doctorate Recipients (NRC).

ties receiving the highest degree in S/E grew by 104 percent in the same period, from 613 in 1975 to 1,253 in 1990. The minority proportion of the doctoral population, however, remains disproportionately small. Minorities comprise approximately 20 percent of the total U.S. population (U.S. Bureau of the Census, 1990), and yet they received just 9 percent of the doctoral degrees granted in 1990.

Increases in both the number and share of doctoral degrees are not uniform across all racial or ethnic groups and fields. African Americans, compared to Asians, Hispanics, and Native Americans, experienced a modest growth in the number and proportion of Ph.D.'s received between 1975 and 1990. During the sixteen-year period, the number of Ph.D. degrees awarded to African Americans increased from 261 to 308, and their share of doctorates grew from 1.9 to 2.1 percent.

On the other hand, among those groups who made significant gains, Native Americans had the largest growth in both number and proportion of doctorates received, followed by Hispanics and Asians. Native Americans demonstrated the biggest gains in life sciences, Hispanics in physical sciences, and Asians in psychology.[8]

Women have made great strides in S/E doctoral education. In 1975, 17 percent of the doctoral recipients were women, whereas 36 percent of doctoral recipients were women in 1990. Moreover, their participation reached a record-level high in 1990. The number of women earning the Ph.D. increased 108 percent, from 2,533 in 1975 to 5,269 in 1990. In contrast, the number of men obtaining doctorates declined nearly 22 percent, from 11,942 in 1975 to 9,127 in 1985. This downward trend was halted from 1986 to 1990 when degree production rose from 9,127 to 9,385. It would seem that women are making some progress in S/E training at the highest educational level.

Area of Specialization

Despite minor shifts in field concentration over the years, substantial racial and gender differences in field distribution remain within the doctoral population. In 1990, the index of dissimilarity for African Americans and whites in S/E doctoral training was 27, indicating that 27 percent of African American doctorates in S/E would have to change fields to be distributed in the same manner as white doctorates.[9]

The index of dissimilarity is the lowest between Hispanics and whites. In 1990, only 11 percent of Hispanic S/E doctorates would have to change disciplines to be equally distributed with whites.

Psychology continues to be the favorite discipline of S/E doctorate receipt for African Americans. The proportion of African Americans earning Ph.D.'s in psychology increased from 24 percent in 1975 to 36 percent in 1990.

Table 6.2. Educational Background of Parents of Doctorates in Science and Engineering, 1975–1990

Year and Parents' Degree	Men	Women	Total*	Native Americans	Asians	African Americans	Hispanics	Whites
1975 (all fields)	11,942	2,533	14,475	14	201	261	137	13,240
Total	39%	50%	41%	43%	67%	28%	36%	42%
Ph.D./master's/professional	18%	26%	20%	7%	23%	12%	16%	20%
Baccalaureate	20%	24%	21%	36%	43%	16%	20%	22%
1980 (all fields)	10,259	3,475	13,734	28	329	281	174	12,143
Total	46%	52%	47%	43%	49%	30%	39%	48%
Ph.D./master's/professional	23%	28%	24%	25%	22%	15%	23%	25%
Baccalaureate	23%	24%	23%	18%	26%	15%	16%	23%
1985 (all fields)	9,127	4,246	13,373	42	380	293	254	12,048
Total	53%	56%	54%	55%	59%	29%	48%	55%
Ph.D./master's/professional	29%	31%	30%	21%	33%	17%	27%	30%
Baccalaureate	24%	24%	24%	33%	26%	12%	21%	25%
1990 (all fields)	9,358	5,269	14,627	41	508	308	396	13,111
Total	58%	57%	58%	37%	58%	34%	42%	59%
Ph.D./master's/professional	37%	37%	37%	17%	39%	23%	28%	38%
Baccalaureate	21%	20%	21%	20%	19%	11%	14%	21%

Note: Data are for doctorates with at least one parent who had a baccalaureate, graduate, or professional degree.
*Includes doctorates with unknown race/ethnicity categories.
Source: The Survey of Earned Doctorates and the Survey of Doctorate Recipients (NRC).

Doctorates awarded to Asians continue to cluster in mathematics, computer sciences, and engineering (MCSE), their traditional stronghold in S/E at all educational levels. In 1990, more than one-third of the S/E doctorates awarded to native-born and naturalized Asians were in MCSE. This is significant in light of their relatively low proportion in the U.S. population, notwithstanding the number of degrees earned by permanent residents and foreign students of Asian descent. Compared with other minorities, a larger number of Asian doctorates will be available to meet both the replacement and new demands for highly trained workers in these rapidly expanding industries.

Hispanics, unlike African Americans and Asians, have a more even distribution across disciplines. In 1990, one-half of the Ph.D.'s granted to Hispanics were in either the life sciences or psychology.

The trends of overall increases of female participation in S/E doctoral education obscures a huge gender difference in area of specialization. In 1990, 29 percent of female doctorates would have to change areas of specialization in order to have distributions identical to male doctorates. Variations in early socialization and educational experiences are largely responsible for such a high degree of field differentiation between the sexes (see Vetter, Chapter 1 above). And, although the largest growth in the number of Ph.D.'s granted to women was in MCSE, only one of thirteen female doctorates obtained their degrees in these fields, in contrast to one in four among male doctorates. The trends of female representation in doctoral training in MCSE, though remarkable, suggest that it will take a considerable amount of time and extraordinary effort for women to catch up with men in these fields (Dix, 1987b; Etzkowitz et al.; Chapter 3 above; Mcilwee and Robinson, 1992; Society of Women Engineers, 1985).

Educational Background of Parents

It has been argued that the occupational status of parents, along with their educational levels, is one of the most reliable predictors of the academic achievements of the next generation (Featherman and Hauser, 1978). However, the data in table 6.2 offer mixed support for these views. The number of S/E doctorate recipients who report having at least one parent with a college degree has increased gradually since 1975, especially among African Americans and whites. Since 1985, all doctorates, except Native Americans, are more likely to have a parent with a graduate or professional degree rather than a baccalaureate.

However, the proportion of minority group members with Ph.D.'s and having parents who graduated from college varies enormously across groups. In fact, racial differences in the proportion of post–college–educated parents observed in 1990 correspond closely with the relative share

Table 6.3. Source of Support of Doctorates in Science and Engineering with U.S. Citizenship, by Gender and Race/Ethnicity, 1975–1990

Year and Source of Support*	Men	Women	Total†	Native Americans	Asians	African Americans	Hispanics	Whites
1975 (all fields)	11,664	2,471	14,135	14	198	256	137	13,126
Federal	57%	58%	57%	64%	41%	56%	50%	58%
Loans	18%	15%	18%	21%	16%	30%	26%	17%
Personal	65%	64%	65%	64%	60%	65%	70%	65%
University	82%	76%	81%	71%	82%	72%	73%	81%
Other	12%	12%	12%	7%	11%	22%	19%	12%
1980 (all fields)	10,018	3,401	13,419	28	328	277	169	12,028
Federal	36%	37%	37%	36%	27%	41%	35%	37%
Loans	18%	21%	19%	25%	16%	36%	30%	19%
Personal	63%	67%	64%	57%	64%	59%	65%	64%
University	82%	74%	80%	82%	79%	64%	73%	80%
Other	9%	11%	10%	7%	12%	27%	21%	9%
1985 (all fields)	8,978	4,183	13,161	42	374	288	252	11,987
Federal	24%	29%	25%	31%	24%	39%	33%	25%
Loans	34%	38%	36%	45%	32%	44%	51%	35%
Personal	75%	80%	77%	71%	67%	74%	79%	77%
University	86%	80%	84%	86%	85%	73%	80%	84%
Other	10%	12%	11%	12%	10%	17%	17%	11%
1990 (all fields)	9,048	5,090	14,138	40	492	286	385	12,738
Federal	17%	22%	19%	20%	18%	27%	28%	18%
Loans	36%	41%	38%	48%	28%	52%	48%	38%
Personal	70%	79%	73%	75%	62%	72%	69%	74%
University	86%	81%	84%	65%	85%	81%	82%	84%
Other	14%	16%	15%	28%	17%	24%	18%	14%

Note: Data exclude doctorates who did not report source of support.
*Doctorates may have had multiple sources of support.
†Includes doctorates with unknown race/ethnicity categories.
Source: The Survey of Earned Doctorates and the Survey of Doctorate Recipients (NRC).

of each minority group in the doctoral population. For example, among minorities, not only did Asians have the largest share of S/E Ph.D.'s, but 39 percent of the Asian doctorates had a parent with an advanced degree. Similarly, 28 percent of the parents of Hispanic doctorates, who represented the second largest minority group receiving Ph.D.'s, had graduate or professional education in 1990, compared to only 23 percent among African American doctorates.

The SED data provide some support for the proposition of intergenerational transmission in higher education, at least among minorities. Although whites were as likely as Asians to have parents at all educational levels, the absolute and relative numbers of white doctorates have declined since 1975. This indicates that the strength of association for whites between parents' educational background and academic aspirations may be weaker than that for Asians.

A major similarity shared between male and female doctorates is that parents of recent graduates today are better educated than those in previous decades. Throughout the sixteen-year period of our analysis, the average proportion of female doctorates having at least one college-educated parent was 54 percent compared to 49 percent among male Ph.D.'s.

What is also interesting is that female graduates showed the highest percentage with educated parents at all levels between 1975 and 1985. The dramatic growth in both the number and share of women in the S/E doctoral population since 1975 underscores the importance of parental influence in the pursuit of the Ph.D. for women.

Sources of Financial Support

The data in table 6.3 show that university support has been the major source of funding for all groups. Regardless of racial or ethnic background and gender, doctorate recipients felt the impact of declining federal funding for higher education. This reduction is followed by corresponding increases in loans and other sources of financial assistance. These changes have had a much greater impact on African Americans and Hispanics than on other groups in terms of seeking alternate means of support and, therefore, reducing the overall amount of debt upon graduation.

During the sixteen-year period, the proportions of African Americans and Hispanics seeking loans for support were far greater than that of other groups. In 1990, 52 percent of African Americans and 48 percent of Hispanics, in contrast to 28 percent of Asians and 38 percent of whites, cited loans as one of their major sources of funding. These data suggest that a higher percentage of African American and Hispanic graduates had incurred more debts than Asians and whites by the time they entered the job market.

Table 6.4. Median Number of Years to Doctoral Degree for U.S. Citizens, by Gender, Race/Ethnicity, and Field, 1975–1990

Year and Field	Men	Women	Total*	Native Americans	Asians	African Americans	Hispanics	Whites
1975 (all fields)	7.1	7.3	7.1	7.1	9.2	8.7	7.8	7.1
Physical sciences	6.5	6.3	6.5	NC‡	7.9	9.8	8.3	6.4
MCSE†	7.4	7.2	7.4	7	12.1	9.3	8	7.3
Life sciences	6.9	7	6.7	NC	6.7	10	7	6.9
Psychology	6.8	7.1	6.9	7.8	5.3	6.9	6.5	6.8
Social sciences	8.4	8.6	8.4	6.8	11.7	8.8	8.8	8.4
1980 (all fields)	7.3	8.1	7.5	7.3	8.9	9	8.3	7.4
Physical sciences	6.4	6.1	6.4	6	7.6	8.8	8.6	6.4
MCSE†	7.3	7.6	7.3	8	11.9	8.5	7.1	7.2
Life sciences	6.9	7.7	7.1	6.3	7.9	10.1	7.9	7.1
Psychology	7.7	8.3	7.9	6.5	7.5	8.6	7.7	7.9
Social sciences	9.1	9.7	9.3	11	13.1	9.3	10.3	9.2
1985 (all fields)	7.9	9.1	8.2	8.5	8.2	10.3	8.5	8.2
Physical sciences	6.6	6.6	6.6	7.5	7.3	7.3	6.4	6.6
MCSE†	7.6	7.1	7.5	NC	7.8	10.5	8	7.5
Life sciences	7.8	9	8.1	8.3	8.2	9.3	7.9	8
Psychology	9.5	9.5	9.5	7.5	8.5	10	9.5	9.5
Social sciences	10.2	11.6	10.7	18.5	12	12	9.9	10.6
1990 (all fields)	8.3	9.8	8.8	12.3	8.1	10.9	9.2	8.7
Physical sciences	6.9	6.8	6.9	11	6.5	8.2	7	6.8
MCSE†	7.9	8.5	8	8	8.1	8.6	9.5	8
Life sciences	8.4	9.9	9	9.3	8.3	10.2	9.1	9
Psychology	10.3	10.2	10.2	16.5	8.9	11	8.5	10.3
Social sciences	11	12.5	11.7	15	11.5	13.7	12.1	11.5

Note: Data are median years from baccalaureate to doctorate.
* Includes doctorates with unknown race/ethnicity categories.
† Mathematics, computer sciences, and engineering.
‡ NC, no cases.

To a certain extent, this unique pattern of support is related to field distribution (NRC, 1991b). Due to their concentration in physical sciences and MCSE, Asian doctorates have traditionally relied on university funding as the principal means of their support. These disciplines are more likely to receive long-term lucrative R&D contracts from both the public and private sectors. In contrast, a stronger orientation among African Americans and Hispanics to psychology and the social sciences, fields which receive less external funding than the natural sciences and engineering, partially explains their greater dependence on loans and other sources of funds. Besides, a strong presence of foreign students in physical sciences and MCSE might have increased the competition for financial aid and thereby lowers the overall chances of getting university support among minority doctorates (Blum, 1992).

Gender differences in financial support for doctoral training for the period under review were not as large as that among Asians, African Americans, Hispanics, and whites. However, among recent graduates, men were still more likely to indicate university funding as their main source of assistance, while women tended to rely on loans and personal funds. As a result, a large number of female doctorates will have a greater burden of debt than their male counterparts upon completion of their graduate training. The modest gender variation in the type of funding can be largely attributed to differences in field concentration.

Time to the Doctorate

The time it takes to complete doctoral training after college graduation, as shown in table 6.4, varies by race or ethnicity, gender, and field.[10] When other groups increased their time to complete their doctoral requirements, the median years to degree for Asians dropped from 9.2 in 1975 to 8.1 in 1990. This represents the shortest time interval for all groups. In contrast, African Americans and Native Americans had the longest time-to-degree in the doctoral population. The median years to degree had increased from 8.7 in 1975 to 10.9 in 1990 for African Americans and from 7.1 in 1975 to 12.3 in 1990 for Native Americans. Even in fields with a relatively shorter time-to-degree, such as physical sciences and MCSE, these two groups still take more time than Asians to complete their graduate training. In 1990, the median years for African Americans to complete their doctorate requirements in physical sciences and MCSE were 8.2 and 8.6, respectively. The median time-to-degree for Native Americans in these respective fields was 11 and 8 years.

In psychology and the social sciences, the total time elapsed between baccalaureate and doctorate is shorter among Asians than among African Americans. The racial gap can be attributed in part to a higher representation of Asians in economics. A decline in federal assistance for higher education in the last decade may be a critical factor for why it takes African Americans longer to complete their graduate training (Mercer, 1992; Sigelman and Welch, 1991; Thomas, 1990). A large number of African Americans and Hispanics have to rely on other means for their educational support, thereby increasing attrition rates and prolonging the length of time it takes to obtain their degrees. Taken together, these inadequate resources have adversely affected the production of minority Ph.D. scientists and engineers (Dix, 1987a; Pearson and Bechtel, 1989; Smith, 1991).

The gender gap in time-to-degree has increased substantially, from 0.2 median years in 1975 to 1.5 median years in 1990. Again, the declining federal support for higher education may be causing greater difficulties for women than men to secure other sources of financial aid. Like non-Asian minorities, female doctorates also take considerable time to finish their degree.

The increasing gender gap in time-to-degree may reflect a growing presence of women with family obligations in the S/E doctoral population. The dramatic increase in female participation in graduate training in recent years suggests that marriage and child care responsibilities might prolong the time-to-degree for women doctorates. However, evidence for this issue is not conclusive. Some scholars found that family responsibilities do not interfere with women's pursuit in advanced studies (Cole, 1987; Cole and Zuckerman, 1991). Some argue that being married does not necessarily reduce the research productivity of female Ph.D.'s. Quite the contrary, married women might have more resources and larger networks at their disposal than their single female counterparts (Astin and Davis, 1985).

It should also be noted that the pattern of time-to-degree across fields for female doctorates is very similar to that for male Ph.D.'s. For instance, both men and women obtained their highest degree in the physical sciences in less than seven years in 1990. However, in life sciences, the median years to doctorate were 8.4 for men and 9.9 for women. It also took both groups ten to twelve years to complete their doctoral requirements in psychology and the social sciences.

Postdoctoral Opportunities

Table 6.5 summarizes the postgraduation plans for doctorate recipients by gender and race or ethnicity from 1975 to 1990. Although more than two-thirds of doctorates reported having definite career plans upon graduation, the proportion of doctorates with commitments has declined, especially among non-Asian minorities. In 1975, for example, three out of four African Americans, Hispanics, and Native Americans had postgraduation career plans. By 1990, only two out of three made similar responses. This may be an indication of a greater degree of career uncertainty among non-Asian minority Ph.D.'s, despite alleged increasing efforts to recruit highly educated minorities into academe and in industry (United States Congress, 1990).

The trends toward postgraduate career plans may in fact be related to a glut of tenured faculty who are not retiring as previously predicted (Bowen and Sosa, 1989). Another explanation may be that corporate merging and downsizing (e.g., General Motors, IBM, and Westinghouse) may affect the way new Ph.D.'s are making career plans. Finally, foreign-born U.S.-trained doctorates have become an attractive and convenient source of Ph.D.'s for employers (NRC, 1988). Their strong presence in doctoral programs, especially in MCSE, intensifies job competition for higher paying scientific or technical jobs in the United States.

Another interesting characteristic is the increasing incidence of postdoctoral study rather than immediate employment. Asian doctorates are more likely to go on for postdoctoral training than African Americans, Hispanics, Native Americans, and whites. Part of the racial differences in postgraduate career plans may be due to variations in field concentration, rather than to market demands in different specialties.

What is just as interesting is the declining incidence of academic employment, especially among minorities. However, African Americans and Hispanics report the highest proportion of academic employment. Conversely, Asians opted for self-employment or work in the industrial sector.

Furthermore, civil service employment has little appeal to minority Ph.D.'s.[11] The shrinking college-age population may be part of the reason for an overall decline of interest and opportunities in academic appointments (see Vetter, Chapter 1 above). Nonetheless, a relatively larger proportion of African Americans and Hispanics stayed out of industries and business, thus suggesting that, contrary to the highly publicized reports, the private sector has not effectively recruited non-Asian minority talent. In contrast, a greater proportion of Asians and whites reported definite employment plans for industry and business.

According to table 6.5, men are more likely than women to have definite postgraduation *career* plans. Since 1975, there has been a steady growth in the proportion reporting postdoctoral *study* as their postgraduate plans among both men and women. A comparable gender proportion reporting plans for postdoctoral training is inconsistent with the assertion that women have more difficulties than men in obtaining support and re-

Table 6.5. Postgraduation Plans of Doctorates with U.S. Citizenship, by Gender and Race/Ethnicity, 1975–1990

Year and Plan	Men	Women	Total*	Native Americans	Asians	African Americans	Hispanics	Whites
1975+ (all fields)	11,942	2,533	14,475	14	201	261	137	13,240
Definite plans	76%	69%	75%	79%	66%	76%	76%	76%
Study	25%	31%	26%	18%	31%	13%	18%	26%
Employment	74%	69%	73%	82%	67%	86%	81%	73%
Academe	37%	46%	39%	36%	24%	61%	53%	38%
Government	15%	8%	14%	18%	15%	14%	7%	14%
Industry/self-employment	17%	5%	15%	9%	24%	5%	19%	15%
Other/unknown employment	5%	8%	6%	18%	4%	6%	2%	6%
Other plans	1%	1%	1%	0%	2%	1%	1%	1%
1980+ (all fields)	10,259	3,475	13,734	28	329	281	174	12,143
Definite plans	78%	71%	76%	75%	74%	72%	70%	77%
Study	31%	33%	32%	24%	35%	14%	20%	32%
Employment	69%	66%	68%	76%	65%	85%	80%	68%
Academe	29%	36%	31%	43%	18%	51%	43%	30%
Government	13%	8%	12%	5%	8%	16%	14%	12%
Industry/self-employment	21%	12%	19%	24%	33%	5%	15%	19%
Other/unknown employment	6%	11%	7%	5%	5%	12%	8%	7%
Other plans	0%	0%	0%	0%	0%	1%	0%	0%
1985+ (all fields)	9,127	4,246	13,373	42	380	293	254	12,048
Definite plans	75%	69%	73%	74%	66%	61%	70%	74%
Study	35%	35%	35%	29%	41%	18%	26%	35%
Employment	65%	65%	65%	71%	58%	81%	73%	65%
Academe	26%	31%	27%	35%	18%	38%	38%	27%
Government	10%	10%	10%	10%	7%	16%	9%	10%
Industry/self-employment	24%	14%	21%	16%	31%	12%	16%	21%
Other/unknown employment	5%	11%	7%	19%	2%	14%	10%	7%
Other plans	0%	0%	0%	0%	0%	1%	1%	0%

1990+ (all fields)	9,358	5,269	14,627	41	508	308	396	13,111
Definite plans	73%	69%	72%	63%	66%	66%	66%	73%
Study	37%	38%	37%	27%	43%	20%	31%	37%
Employment	63%	62%	63%	73%	57%	79%	69%	62%
Academe	24%	30%	26%	50%	14%	46%	34%	25%
Government	10%	7%	9%	0%	8%	10%	11%	9%
Industry/self-employment	25%	15%	21%	15%	31%	10%	15%	21%
Other/unknown employment	5%	10%	7%	8%	4%	12%	9%	7%
Other plans	0%	0%	0%	0%	0%	1%	0%	0%

* Includes doctorates with unknown race/ethnicity categories.
† Number of doctorates who responded to the question on postgraduation plans.

Table 6.6. Employment Rates for Doctoral Scientists and Engineers with U.S. Citizenship, by Gender, Race/Ethnicity, and Field, 1989

Number (%) of Those in Each Field	Men	Women	Total*	Native Americans	Asians	African Americans	Hispanics	Whites
Index of Dissimilarity (D)†	[33]			[13]	[24]	[20]	[5]	
Physical sciences	95,139	8,477	103,616	186	7,062	696	1,382	93,844
	(92)	(89)	(91)	(100)	(96)	(98)	(92)	(91)
MCSE‡	83,360	3,964	87,324	82	11,685	766	1,180	73,451
	(1)	(95)	(94)	(85)	(98)	(76)	(96)	(94)
Life sciences	94,130	26,004	120,134	196	6,458	1,562	1,660	109,850
	(91)	(90)	(90)	(87)	(96)	(94)	(95)	(90)
Psychology	43,162	24,104	67,266	127	988	1,441	1,367	63,257
	(94)	(93)	(94)	(97)	(94)	(97)	(95)	(94)
Social sciences	46,114	12,445	58,559	162	2,154	1,372	876	53,862
	(91)	(91)	(91)	(98)	(90)	(95)	(97)	(91)
Total	361,905	74,994	436,899	753	28,347	5,837	6,465	394,264
	(92)	(91)	(92)	(94)	(96)	(93)	(95)	(92)

Note: Data parentheses show the percentage of those employed full-time to the total science and engineering labor force with doctorates.

*Includes doctoral scientists and engineers with unknown race/ethnicity categories.

†Percentage of women (or minorities) who would have to change occupational fields to be distributed in the same manner as men (or whites).

‡Mathematics, computer sciences, and engineering.

sources from their mentors or institutions to advance their training and research. This may be largely the result of field effects (Cole, 1979; Weis, 1987; Zuckerman, Cole, and Bruer, 1991).

A more detailed examination of postgraduate career plans reveals that a higher proportion of women report academic appointments than their male counterparts. Again, part of this may be field related. It also suggests that women may be more willing to trade the higher paying, but less secure industrial employment for lower paying and more flexible academic employment. Thus, self-selection may be one of the factors in explaining the gender gap in employment plans.

Career Prospects for Minority and Women Ph.D.'s

Although the proportion of doctorates with definite career plans has declined gradually in the last sixteen years, the outlook for doctoral scientists and engineers in the job market remains bright.[12] Table 6.6 provides a summary of employment rates in major fields in 1989. In 1989, more than 90 percent of doctoral scientists and engineers were employed full-time. The possible future shortage of scientific and engineering personnel suggests that the career prospects for doctoral scientists and engineers will be improved.

Full-time employment rates for minority Ph.D.'s is highest among Asians. In 1989, 96 percent of the Asian doctoral S/E work force held full-time jobs, compared to 95 percent of Hispanics and 94 percent of Native Americans. During the same period, 93 percent of African Americans and 92 percent of whites with Ph.D.'s occupied full-time positions.

On the other hand, there is substantial occupational field segregation by race in the Ph.D. S/E work force. The index of dissimilarity indicates that 24 percent of Asians would have to switch their fields in order to be equally distributed with whites. It is also important to note that the level of field segregation between Asians and whites was higher in the job market than in doctoral education. In 1990, only 17 percent Asians would have to change their field of doctoral training to be equally distributed with their white counterparts.

Asian doctorates in S/E, more so than non-Asian minorities and women, may experience more restrictions in the labor market. It is possible that Asians may have stronger preference for science-based or technically oriented fields (Hsia, 1988; Leong, 1991). Thus, a larger proportion of them practiced in quantitative or engineering fields for a longer period of time (Tang, 1991). Unlike other groups, Asians may be more responsive to market changes. Their relatively high rates of full-time employment in MCSE and the physical and life sciences suggest that the relatively high

Table 6.7. Full-Time Employed Doctoral Scientists and Engineers, by Gender, Race/Ethnicity, and Sector, 1989

Field and Sector	Men	Women	Total	Native Americans	Asians	African Americans	Hispanics	Whites
Total*	333,797	68,325	402,122	708	27,293	5,442	6,103	361,536
Academic institutions	49%	54%	50%	56%	39%	60%	52%	51%
Business/industry	34%	26%	33%	23%	47%	22%	29%	32%
Government	10%	8%	10%	15%	9%	11%	11%	10%
Other	6%	12%	7%	6%	4%	7%	8%	7%
Physical sciences	87,059	7,506	94,565	186	6,746	682	1,266	85,289
Academic institutions	39%	45%	40%	44%	32%	47%	53%	40%
Business/industry	47%	40%	46%	29%	56%	37%	33%	46%
Government	10%	10%	10%	24%	9%	15%	12%	10%
Other	4%	6%	4%	3%	4%	1%	2%	4%
MCSE†	78,758	3,748	82,506	70	11,489	581	1,127	69,079
Academic institutions	44%	57%	44%	56%	29%	39%	43%	47%
Business/industry	46%	33%	46%	41%	62%	52%	39%	43%
Government	7%	6%	7%	3%	7%	8%	12%	7%
Other	3%	3%	3%	0%	2%	1%	6%	3%
Life sciences	85,240	23,352	108,592	170	6,194	1,468	1,574	98,876
Academic institutions	58%	64%	59%	45%	54%	65%	63%	60%
Business/industry	23%	18%	22%	32%	26%	13%	18%	22%
Government	13%	9%	12%	16%	13%	14%	13%	12%
Other	6%	9%	7%	7%	7%	8%	5%	7%
Psychology	40,734	22,451	63,185	123	925	1,401	1,301	59,373
Academic institutions	44%	41%	43%	40%	52%	56%	36%	42%
Business/industry	32%	34%	32%	21%	20%	19%	36%	33%
Government	8%	6%	7%	16%	14%	12%	8%	7%
Other	17%	19%	18%	23%	14%	13%	20%	18%
Social sciences	42,006	11,268	53,274	159	1,939	1,310	835	48,919
Academic institutions	70%	67%	69%	94%	72%	73%	68%	69%
Business/industry	13%	14%	13%	0%	13%	14%	17%	13%
Government	11%	9%	11%	6%	12%	6%	11%	11%
Other	6%	10%	7%	0%	3%	7%	5%	7%

*Includes doctorates with unknown race/ethnicity categories.
†Mathematics, computer sciences, and engineering.

level of occupational field segregation observed between Asians and whites may be driven by market demands rather than by market constraints.

By contrast, field segregation between African Americans and whites was lower in the job market than in doctoral training. In 1989, only 20 percent of African American S/E doctorates would have to change occupational field in order to have the same occupational distribution of whites, compared to 27 percent in doctoral education. A higher degree of occupational assimilation for African American doctorates offers further evidence that Asian doctorates have stronger field preference than other minority Ph.D.'s.

Another area of concern is the low African American full-time employment rate in MCSE. Only three-quarters of those in MCSE were able to find full-time jobs in 1989. It is an indication that a larger proportion of African Americans with doctoral training are underemployed.[13]

A careful examination of the minority proportion in MCSE provides some support for Kanter's (1977) notion of "token status." She postulates that minorities and women are most vulnerable when their numbers are relatively small in a profession or in an organization. The positive linkage between comparative group size and full-time employment rates for minorities found in MCSE, but not in other S/E fields, suggests that despite what seems to be a high demand for personnel in MCSE, doctoral minorities with a relatively small proportion may be in a somewhat disadvantaged position in competing with foreign workers for full-time employment.

The 1989 full-time employment rates for female S/E doctorates were comparable to that of male doctorates. However, men seemed to enjoy more job opportunities in the physical sciences than women. Only 89 percent of female physical scientists worked full-time, compared to 92 percent among males. Furthermore, one-third of women S/E doctorates would have to change their occupational field to be distributed in the same manner as men. Again, the level of field segregation by gender is lower in doctoral training than in the job market. Doctoral women scientists and engineers may have more difficulties finding or keeping full-time jobs in their field of expertise.

Employment Sector

Table 6.7 summarizes the sectoral distribution of full-time employed doctoral scientists and engineers in 1989. The racial pattern of sectoral employment for doctoral scientists and engineers was similar to that of their postgraduation employment plans. While the majority of Hispanics, Native Americans, African Americans, and women held academic positions, nearly one-half of all Asian S/E doctorates were employed in business and industry. This unique sectoral distribution among Asians is

largely field-related. Moreover, Asians are more likely to hold nonacademic jobs in higher-paying, high-demand fields such as the physical sciences and MCSE than in the life and social sciences and psychology.

In contrast, due to the nature of disciplines, the largest employer for
doctoral social scientists and psychologists, regardless of racial or ethnic
background, are academic institutions. Thus, the career prospects of these
doctorates are more likely to be affected by demographic changes. A
shrinking college-age population, along with large reductions in federal
and state funding for higher education, may have a larger impact on social
scientists and psychologists than on those in physical sciences or MCSE.
Unless there is an expansion in the public sector, job competition among
Ph.D.'s in the social sciences and psychology will remain intense.

Sectoral employment distribution also varies by gender. Women are
more likely to hold full-time academic jobs than men in MCSE and the
physical and life sciences. The trend is in reverse in psychology and the
social sciences.

Academic Ph.D.'s: Tenure and Rank

Data in table 6.8 show that the majority of academically employed doctoral scientists and engineers are tenured. Overall, similar proportions of
whites, African Americans, Asians, and Native Americans, aggregate over
all fields, hold tenure status. Nonetheless, there are racial differences
across disciplines in terms of job security and prestige.

Although Asians are overrepresented in the physical sciences and
MCSE, they are less likely than other minority groups—African Americans and Hispanics—to be in tenure positions. This may reflect, in part,
their recent entry to these fields. Alternatively, many Asians may not stay
in academe long enough before they move on to more lucrative private
sector employment (Tang, 1993). Many academically employed Asians in
the physical sciences and MCSE may not have long-term career commitments. By contrast, despite their underrepresentation in these fields, African Americans tend to choose and remain in academe. Besides, eight out of
every ten Asians and seven of ten African Americans, compared to only
four of ten whites, were tenured in the social sciences. This suggests that
minority faculty in these specialties are generally older than whites.

There is some indication that Asians and Hispanics are in more disadvantaged positions than African Americans and whites in academe. The
two former groups are more likely to hold non–tenure-track jobs. In 1989,
a quarter of Asians in MCSE and another third in the physical and life
sciences were instructors or occupied positions that do not have any prospects for permanent employment. Nearly 40 percent of all Hispanics in the
life sciences and psychology were not in tenure-track positions.

Table 6.8. Academically Full-Time Employed Doctoral Scientists and Engineers, by Gender, Race/Ethnicity, Rank, and Field, 1989

Tenure Status and Field	Men	Women	Total	Native Americans	Asians	African Americans	Hispanics	Whites
Tenured	65	40	61	53	60	58	51	61
Physical sciences	65	38	63	87	51	70	75	63
MCSE†	70	50	69	14	66	69	72	69
Life sciences	59	33	54	45	52	54	40	54
Psychology	63	41	56	0	44	38	37	57
Social sciences	72	51	67	63	80	70	40	67
Tenure track	13	22	15	26	13	21	22	15
Physical sciences	11	19	12	3	16	18	10	11
MCSE†	14	30	15	77	10	18	15	16
Life sciences	14	24	16	31	11	23	22	16
Psychology	13	19	15	0	24	30	25	15
Social sciences	14	22	15	30	15	14	39	15
Other/Non-tenure track	21	37	24	21	27	21	26	24
Physical sciences	24	42	26	10	33	12	15	26
MCSE†	16	21	16	9	24	13	13	16
Life sciences	27	43	30	25	36	23	38	30
Psychology	23	40	29	100	31	31	38	28
Social sciences	15	27	17	7	5	16	22	18
Total*	152,519	32,785	185,304	360	9,907	2,837	2,844	168,879
Physical sciences	29,381	2,852	32,233	77	1,890	257	536	29,242
MCSE†	32,313	2,023	34,336	35	3,121	216	454	30,464
Life sciences	46,489	13,230	59,719	65	3,163	808	934	54,624
Psychology	15,834	7,577	23,411	40	407	646	365	21,920
Social sciences	28,502	7,103	35,605	143	1,326	910	555	32,629

Note: Totals are given as numbers; all other figures are given as percentages.
* Includes scientists and engineers with unknown race/ethnicity categories.
†Mathematics, computer sciences, and engineering.

The career patterns of minority academics suggest that African Americans and Native Americans are more secure than their Asian and Hispanic counterparts in terms of holding tenure status or at least that they are employed in tenure-track positions. However, it should be noted that African American and Hispanic academics are concentrated in traditionally African American and Hispanic institutions. A relatively small proportion of African American and Hispanic S/E doctorates, when compared with their Asian counterparts, are employed in major research universities (de la Luz Reyes and Halcon, 1991; Jackson, 1991).

Among doctoral scientists and engineers, men are more likely than women to be tenured. In 1989, two-thirds of men held tenure compared to only 40 percent of women. In contrast, however, a larger proportion of women than men were either in tenure-track or non–tenure-track positions. This gender-specific career pattern holds across fields. The gender gap in tenure status may be partly attributed to differences in experience.

Table 6.9. Tenured Doctoral Faculty, by Rank and Field, 1989

Rank and Field	Men	Women	Total	Native Americans	Asians	African Americans	Hispanics	Whites
Full professor	70	45	67	49	73	41	59	68
Physical sciences	77	58	76	52	85	58	82	76
MCSE†	70	45	69	0	64	55	54	70
Life sciences	69	42	65	93	75	42	59	65
Psychology	68	43	62	NC‡	67	30	39	63
Social sciences	66	48	64	36	78	38	35	64
Associate professor	28	49	31	50	27	52	38	30
Physical sciences	21	38	22	48	13	14	17	22
MCSE†	28	48	29	100	36	41	46	28
Life sciences	30	52	33	0	25	56	37	33
Psychology	29	50	34	NC	29	62	54	33
Social sciences	32	50	35	64	22	60	58	34
Assistant professor	2	5	2	1	1	6	3	2
Physical sciences	2	4	2	0	2	27	1	2
MCSE†	1	7	2	0	0	4	0	2
Life sciences	1	6	2	7	0	2	4	2
Psychology	3	7	4	NC	4	8	7	4
Social sciences	2	2	2	0	0	3	7	2
Total*	98,839	13,065	111,904	191	5,868	1,654	1,433	102,522
Physical sciences	18,891	1,062	19,953	67	931	180	384	18,278
MCSE†	22,467	1,000	23,467	5	2,067	150	326	20,881
Life sciences	27,244	4,379	31,623	29	1,640	440	371	29,116
Psychology	9,911	3,071	12,982	0	175	248	135	12,395
Social sciences	20,326	3,553	23,879	90	1,055	636	217	21,852

Note: Totals are given as numbers; all other figures are given as percentages.
* Includes doctoral scientists and engineers with unknown race/ethnicity categories.
† Mathematics, computer sciences, and engineering.
‡ No cases.

However, many researchers have documented the hurdles Ph.D. women have to clear in order to achieve academic status similar to that of men with comparable qualifications and productivity (Cole and Fiorentine, 1991; Epstein, 1991; Rosenfeld, 1984).

In addition to tenure status, academic rank is a major indicator of career success for academic scientists and engineers. Table 6.9 provides a distribution of academic rank of doctoral scientists and engineers in four-year colleges and universities by gender and race or ethnicity. Among those with tenure, Asians and Hispanics tend to hold full professorships, especially in the physical sciences. By contrast, tenured African American faculty are more likely to occupy lower academic ranks in every field than their Asian and Hispanic peers. In 1989, among tenured faculty, 73 percent of Asians and 59 percent of Hispanics, compared to 41 percent of African Americans and 49 percent of Native Americans, were full professors.

This trend suggests slower promotion rates for African Americans. As a group, not only do African American faculty hold less prestigious academic positions, but they command fewer resources to increase their reputation, advance careers, and set examples for the next generation (Brown and Clewell, 1991).

Among tenured faculty in four-year colleges and universities, men are more likely than women to be full professors. Surprisingly, this pattern remains the same even in fields where women have relatively high representation in doctoral training. In 1989, less than half of all female doctoral scientists and engineers with tenure held full professorships in psychology or the social sciences, compared to two-thirds among males. Experience apparently explains a portion of the gender disparity in academic rank. Research productivity, however, may not be a major contributing factor for lower promotion rates for female faculty to the highest academic rank (Brush, 1991; Cole, 1987; Smith and Pearson, 1989). There is no strong evidence that married women with children are less productive than single women without family responsibilities (Cole and Zuckerman, 1991; Smith and Pearson, 1989). These data should be encouraging to women scientists and engineers, because more of them plan to enter academia upon completion of their doctoral training. When more male academics approach retiring age, coupled with an anticipated growth in faculty positions generated by the enrollment surge expected in the late 1990s (Bowen and Schuster, 1986; Bowen and Sosa, 1989; Solomon and Wingard, 1991), increasing female participation in doctoral S/E training and in teaching will ensure their growing influence in academia.

Salaries by Employment Sector

The median annual earnings of full-time employed doctoral scientists and engineers by gender and race or ethnicity are summarized in table 6.10. The private sector offers the highest economic returns to doctoral training ($62,489), followed by federal agencies ($54,411). MCSE are the highest paying fields for all doctoral scientists and engineers, except Hispanics. In 1989, the median annual salary for doctorates in MCSE was $61,898. Asians in MCSE employed by business or industry reported the highest median salaries ($62,102), while Asian academic psychologists reported the lowest median earnings ($42,104).

Psychology offers both the highest and lowest salaries for African Americans, ranging from $63,867 to $41,672. The annual median income of African American psychologists in business or industry was 35 percent higher than in academia. However, the largest earnings gap by field and sector was found among Hispanics. In 1989, the median salary for Hispanics working for the private sector in MCSE was $72,596, compared to

Table 6.10. Median Annual Salaries of Full-Time Employed Doctoral Scientists and Engineers, by Gender, Race/Ethnicity, Field, and Sector, 1989

Field and Sector	Men	Women	Total*	Native Americans	Asians	African Americans	Hispanics	Whites
Physical sciences†	59,256	48,095	58,164	51,450	59,268	55,517	58,825	58,204
4-year college or university	55,041	42,218	53,816		58,354	51,796	55,950	53,875
Business and industry	62,692	52,024	61,855		60,270	57,700	62,200	62,445
Federal government	55,015	45,909	53,933		50,557	61,250	54,825	54,669
State and local government	40,905	37,825	40,820					40,863
MCSE†‡	62,381	51,512	61,898	62,450	60,710	61,987	58,258	62,264
4-year college or university	60,517	48,402	59,820		59,895	59,950	55,412	59,908
Business and industry	66,504	57,527	66,181		62,102	62,775	72,596	67,769
Federal government	60,323	50,250	60,237		60,059			60,396
State and local government	50,580		50,580					51,575
Life sciences†	52,696	42,843	50,652	53,450	51,030	46,873	48,798	50,684
4-year college or university	51,361	41,658	48,870		52,450	45,886	44,460	48,824
Business and industry	58,760	50,062	56,747		55,747	59,700	50,863	57,004
Federal government	52,646	44,010	51,160		43,232	50,117		52,458
State and local government	40,849	40,750	40,831					40,830
Psychology†	51,710	44,545	50,138	48,686	46,200	44,495	45,621	50,267
4-year college or university	48,857	40,707	46,794		42,104	41,672	36,719	47,115
Business and industry	70,371	59,983	65,292		60,888	63,867	70,436	65,261
Federal government	50,762	45,473	50,522					50,618
State and local government	45,111	43,650	44,480		48,587	43,150	41,950	44,520
Social sciences†	53,143	45,381	51,179	49,988		47,488		51,662
4-year college or university	51,313	45,193	50,234	48,423	49,713	47,075	40,291	50,534
Business and industry	66,865	50,428	64,682	65,672				65,501
Federal government	60,256	50,756	58,683					58,632
State and local government	45,027	37,488	44,683					44,797
All fields†	56,924	45,116	55,191		57,507	48,579	50,585	55,180
4-year college or university	53,861	42,481	51,746		54,251	46,275	44,965	51,821
Business and industry	64,149	53,055	62,489		60,435	60,348	61,884	62,992
Federal government	55,401	46,003	54,411		50,687	53,006	50,633	54,964
State and local government	44,047	42,166	43,310		40,781	45,057	39,719	43,456

Note: No amount given when sample size is smaller than 20. Data on median annual salaries are not presented in this table. Values are given as dollars.
*Includes doctoral scientists and engineers with unknown race/ethnicity categories.
†Includes 2-year colleges, elementary/secondary schools, hospitals/clinics, and other/unreported sectors.
‡Mathematics, computer sciences, and engineering.

$36,719 for academic psychologists. In general, academic positions in psychology offer the lowest paying employment opportunities for minority Ph.D. recipients.

Male and female psychologists employed in business or industry have the highest earnings among doctoral scientists and engineers. In 1989, the median salaries of psychologists hired by the private sector were $70,371 for men and $59,983 for women. Furthermore, among male doctorates, life scientists working for state or local government reported the lowest median income ($40,849). Among female doctorates, social scientists .employed by state or local government received the lowest median salaries ($37,488).

Nonetheless, data in table 6.11 show that not all minority groups fare as well as whites in terms of annual earnings. The median annual salaries for Asians were 104 percent of those for whites. Ironically, the greatest lead for Asians over whites is among academic physical (108 percent) and life (107 percent) scientists. In contrast, Asians generally did poorer than whites in business and industry (96 percent). This can be explained by the fact that a larger proportion of Asian tenured faculty are full professors. Additionally, a relatively large concentration of Asian doctorates, native and foreign born, in the private sector may have increased job competition among themselves.

In 1989, the median incomes for African Americans and Hispanics were 88 and 92 percent of those for whites, respectively. However, the earnings of African Americans were on par with those of whites in MCSE. The greatest median income gap between African Americans and whites was found among physical scientists working for the federal government as well as among academically employed psychologists. The median salary for publicly employed African American physical scientists was about 112 percent of that for salaries of their white colleagues, while it was only 88 percent of that for African American psychologists in four-year colleges and universities.

Earnings ratios between whites and Hispanics vary across fields. Their median earnings in the physical sciences are comparable to one another. However, Hispanics in MCSE (107 percent) and psychology (108 percent) have an economic advantage over whites when they are in business or industry. The largest median earnings gap between these two groups occurred in the social sciences, where Hispanics received only 81 percent of whites' salaries.

Women doctorates earned 79 percent of the salaries of men in science and engineering. The gender gap is largest in the life sciences and smallest in psychology. Among academics, the gap is largest in their underrepresented fields—physical sciences (77 percent) and MCSE (80 percent). Based

Table 6.11. Earnings Ratios of Full-Time Employed Doctoral Scientists and
Engineers, by Gender, Race/Ethnicity, Field, and Sector, 1989

Field and Sector	Women*	Native Americans†	Asians†	African Americans†	Hispanics†
Physical sciences‡	81	88	102	95	101
4-year college or university	77		108	96	104
Business and industry	83		97	92	100
Federal government	83		92	112	100
State and local government	92				
MCSE‡§	83	100	98	100	94
4-year college or university	80		100	100	92
Business and industry	87		92	93	107
Federal government	83		99		
State and local government					
Life sciences‡	81	105	101	92	96
4-year college or university	81		107	94	91
Business and industry	85		98	105	89
Federal government	84		82	96	
State and local government	100				
Psychology‡	86	97	92	89	91
4-year college or university	83		89	88	78
Business and industry	85		93	98	108
Federal government	90				
State and local government	97			97	
Social sciences‡	85		94	92	81
4-year college or university	88		98	93	80
Business and industry	75				
Federal government	84				
State and local government	83				
All fields‡	79	91	104	88	92
4-year college or university	79	93	105	89	87
Business and industry	83	104	96	96	98
Federal government	83		92	96	92
State and local government	96		94	104	91

Note: No amount given when sample size is smaller than 20. Data on earnings ratios are not presented
in this table.
*As a percentage of median salaries of male scientists or engineers.
†As a percentage of median salaries of white scientists or engineers.
‡Includes 2-year colleges, elementary and secondary schools, hospitals and clinics, and other and unre-
ported sectors.
§Mathematics, computer sciences, and engineering.

on these statistics, along with findings of other recent research (Zuckerman, Cole, and Bruer, 1991), given the short tenure of women in these
disciplines, it is just a matter of time before female doctorates reach economic parity with their male counterparts.

Summary and Conclusions

This profile not only updates our knowledge of the recent trends in S/E doctorate production, it also underscores the differences as well as commonalities shared among minority and women Ph.D.'s in education and employment. We can summarize our analysis as follows.

Non-Asian minorities and women are still heavily underrepresented at the highest level of S/E education. Women, however, made relatively more gains in terms of number and proportion than did minority groups between 1975 and 1990. And African Americans had the smallest growth in the minority doctoral population, both in absolute and relative terms.

There is substantial gender and racial or ethnic field segregation among S/E doctorates in education and employment. The degree of field segregation between whites and minorities as well as between males and females is more pronounced in work than in training. Equally important, an increasing proportion of minority and female S/E doctorates have parents with graduate or professional degrees.

Due to gender and racial or ethnic variations in area of specialization, African Americans and women are more inclined to rely on loans or personal monetary sources, rather than university aid, to finance their doctoral training in S/E. This may involve taking more time out and thereby may extend their time for graduation.

The number of minority S/E doctorates with definite career plans is declining. Postdoctoral study has become increasingly popular among minority and women Ph.D.'s. This probably reflects the slow job market. While Asian doctorates are clustered in business and industry, non-Asian minorities and women are more likely to be found in academic settings.

The full-time employment rates in the doctoral S/E work force remain high and they are comparable across groups. Doctoral African Americans and Native Americans in S/E are more likely to hold tenure-track positions or tenure status than their Asian and Hispanic counterparts. However, a larger proportion of tenured Asian and Hispanic faculty occupy higher academic rank than African Americans and Native Americans do. As expected, women S/E doctorates have not caught up with men in getting tenure status or promotion to full professorship.

Finally, the disparity in earnings is larger between males and females than that between whites and minorities. Nonetheless, the private sector clearly has offered minority and women the highest rate of economic returns to doctoral training in S/E. And, minorities have already matched or surpassed the earnings of whites in certain fields and sectors.

Some may interpret these trends as an indication of a lack of strenuous effort on the part of the U.S. government and industry to systematically recruit minorities and women to the highest rank of S/E training. The racial or ethnic and gender inequities in S/E education and employment, ranging from representation, funding, and career paths to earnings, underscore the significance of monitoring their future growth. The analysis we have undertaken herein calls for further research on the sources of differentiation in doctorate attainment.

An optimistic reading of these trends suggests that minorities and women have made inroads in S/E doctoral training. Changing demographics in the United States and multinational economic cooperation will ensure that minorities and women become a larger part of the U.S. doctoral pool. Non-Asian minorities will have the greatest potential for expansion in MCSE, primarily because of their lower employment rates in these areas.

Minority and women S/E doctorates will be a force to be reckoned with in the nation's industrial sector. Of course, their significance in terms of contributions to economic and industrial growth will depend largely on how well we develop and deploy this growing human resource base. This expectation will also depend on how deeply and for how long U.S. industry (e.g., AT&T and Corning) continues to tap into the S/E personnel base from other countries, such as the Commonwealth of the Independent States (the former Soviet Union) and Eastern Europe.

More important, U.S. industry has shown a penchant for recruiting foreign students educated in the United States into their work force. The passage of the 1990 Immigration Act allows employers to triple the number of immigrant scientists and engineers coming into the United States. A larger supply of foreign professionals in the labor markets may affect the annual production of minority and women doctorates. Thus, its potential impact on native-born minority group members and women is an important area of concern for policymakers, educators, and the S/E community.

Notes

For useful suggestions and criticisms, we would like to thank Willie Pearson, Jr., Professor of Sociology at Wake Forest University, and Alan Fechter, Director of the Office of Scientific and Engineering Personnel, National Research Council. We also thank Cheryl B. Leggon, Associate Professor of Sociology, Wake Forest University, and Susan T. Hill, Senior Analyst at the National Science Foundation, for their generous giving of time to our project. Finally, we want to thank Lori Thurgood, Project Manager, National Research Council, and Daniel M. Pasquini,

Research Associate, National Research Council, for their assistance with the data used in the study. None of the individuals or organizations mentioned above bear any responsibility for the work we have produced.

1. This controversial question of a science and engineering (S/E) shortage has received quite a bit of scholarly as well as popular news coverage since Holden's story appeared in *Science* in 1989. Since we do not engage in this debate, we refer readers to the essay by Lederman (1992) and the chapter by Fechter (Chapter 7 below) for an enlarged discussion of this important issue.

2. The SED is an annual survey of new doctoral degree recipients, sponsored by five federal agencies—the National Science Foundation (NSF), the National Institutes of Health (NIH), the U.S. Department of Education (USED), the National Endowment for the Humanities (NEH), and the U.S. Department of Agriculture (USDA)—and conducted by the National Research Council (NRC). The SED does not cover professional degrees (e.g., M.D., D.D.S., O.D., D.V.M., or the J.D.). The SDR is a biennial longitudinal survey of a sample of doctorate population in the United States conducted by the Office of Scientific and Engineering Personnel, National Academy of Sciences for the National Science Foundation since 1973.

3. Both surveys treat Hispanics in aggregate. Variations in socioeconomic background among different groups of the Hispanic population may affect their level of representation in the doctoral population and in the science and engineering work force.

4. We should interpret data for Native Americans with caution, since estimates for degree recipients and for the overall doctoral work force are based on self-declaration of native heritage. Perceptions of an individual's own classification may change over time. It should also be noted that, unlike other minority groups, the size of the doctoral population and work force of Native Americans is very small.

5. Life sciences includes biological and agricultural sciences. Social sciences does not include archeology, communications, history or philosophy of science, linguistics, and public administration.

6. Degrees in the humanities, education, and professional fields are excluded in this analysis.

7. Data for this section are from the SED for 1975, 1980, 1985, and 1990. The data were provided by the Office of Scientific and Engineering Personnel, NRC.

8. We must add a cautionary note here: the number of Native American doctorates in science and engineering is very small. Although we report a proportional increase for Native Americans that appears large, it is derived from *very small* numerical bases. The N's for Native Americans with S/E doctorates in 1975, 1980, 1985, and 1990 are 14, 28, 42, and 41, respectively.

9. The index of dissimilarity *(D)* measures the main dimension of segregation—the degree to which two groups (e.g., African Americans and whites, or Asians and whites, or men and women) are unevenly distributed over a set of categories (e.g., occupation, housing, etc.) (Blalock, 1967). The index of dissimilarity would be zero if there were no segregation between two groups. The formula for D is

$$D = \sum_{i=1}^{n} \frac{|(Bi/B) - (Wi/W)|}{2}$$

where Bi is the number of African Americans in occupation (field) i, B is the total number of African Americans, Wi is the number of whites in occupation (field) i, W is the total number of whites, and n is the number of occupations (fields).

10. Our use of time-to-degree (TTD) refers to total time elapsed between study for the baccalaureate and completion of the doctorate. Other research we have seen in the literature refers to registered-time-to-degree (RTD), which is the time registered in school between the baccalaureate and doctorate (NRC, 1991b; Tuckman, Coyle, and Bae, 1990). One of the better discussions we have seen on this issue is found in Bowen and Rudenstine (1992, pp. 347–59).

11. We could list several reasons for this disinterest in the civil service. Among these would be the long-standing problem of low pay and, more recently, the increased competition for the best jobs.

12. Data for the following sections are from the SDR for 1989, provided by the National Research Council.

13. Underemployment refers to those who are employed part-time but seeking full-time work as well as those who are involuntarily employed outside of their S/E field of expertise (NSF, 1990d, p. 62).

CHAPTER 7

Future Supply and Demand: Cloudy Crystal Balls

Alan Fechter

The entry-level degree for almost all fields of science is usually a doctorate—a requirement that generally takes anywhere from eight to ten years to complete, depending on the field.[1] This relatively long period of training introduces frictions into the labor market for scientists that inhibit the adjustment process to changing demands. Under these circumstances, it might be prudent to try to project the future in order to reduce this friction. Reliable information about future trends in demand could influence students who are contemplating careers and employers of scientists who are contemplating hiring decisions and recruiting strategies to make decisions that might alter supply and demand in anticipation of this future.

Unfortunately, with a few notable exceptions, the track record of such attempts to anticipate future demands leaves much to be desired.[2] The effects of this unsatisfactory performance have been vividly illustrated in recent years, when concerns about impending shortages of trained scientists were expressed, only to be contradicted by a period of limited job opportunities. The result has been a cohort of disappointed new graduates, many of whom enter the labor market only to learn that the years they invested in their training are not bearing the expected fruits of rewarding careers. Some are languishing in postdoctoral appointments, hoping for job opportunities to revive in the future, and many others are settling for jobs outside of science or are seeking training for new careers.

This unfortunate result is not sufficient reason to conclude that we should completely forego efforts to predict trends of supply and demand for people in science. But given the costs of our limited ability to anticipate the future accurately, it would be useful to examine the nature of such efforts and to assess their strengths and weaknesses in order to determine how they might be used in formulating public policy and in assisting private decisionmaking.

My examination will focus on two models: one for doctorates in the natural sciences and engineering produced by the National Science Foundation, and one for arts and sciences faculty developed by William Bowen and Julie Ann Sosa. These models were selected for two reasons: (1) they are comprehensive, covering a wide range of disciplines; and (2) they have been widely cited in the recent policy literature. The former model projects that there will be roughly 9,000 more job openings for doctorates in natural science and engineering fields than degrees produced in these fields by the year 2006. The latter model forecasts shortages of people to fill faculty positions beginning in the late 1990s and extending through the period 2012–17. Counter to prevailing conventional wisdom, the latter model also predicts that recruiting problems will be more serious in the social sciences and humanities than in the natural sciences.

I will examine the strengths and limitations of these models and, based on this assessment, I will evaluate the findings in terms of their policy significance. I conclude (1) that there is a great deal of uncertainty associated with forecasts of supply and demand, and (2) that the models reviewed in this chapter substantially overstate expected shortages. The implications of these conclusions for policy formulation will be discussed. I will describe the numerous mechanisms that exist to bring supply and demand into balance, emphasizing the resource implications associated with using these mechanisms. I will further discuss how policymakers may formulate decisions, given the degree of uncertainty that exists.

Current Conditions

It is difficult to provide an overall evaluation of the current state of the labor market for Ph.D. scientists and engineers. The standard measures of labor market conditions, such as unemployment rates and salary changes, are not quite appropriate. Unemployment rates, for example, are typically well below those experienced by all workers and do not display much variation. Moreover, the sectoral distribution of these scientists differs from that of all workers. Ph.D. scientists are heavily concentrated in academic positions. Thus, academic labor market conditions, which can vary significantly from conditions in other markets, are a strong determinant of the state of labor market conditions for these scientists.

Conditions in academic labor markets vary dramatically by field. In the technologically oriented fields, a substantial fraction of the academic institutions were, until recently, reporting difficulties filling faculty vacancies. In the field of computer science, for example, 38 percent of the institutions reported such difficulty in 1989. In mathematics and engineering, the percentages were 25 and 15, respectively. In contrast, only 11 percent reported recruiting difficulties in arts and humanities (El-Khawas, 1989).

Moreover, there is evidence that some quantitatively oriented fields—engineering, physics, mathematics, and economics—were experiencing difficulties recruiting American students to their graduate programs. Approximately two-fifths to one-half of the students receiving doctorates in these fields were foreign students on temporary visas (NRC, 1993b).[3] Finally, evidence of recruiting difficulties exists in the form of relative faculty salaries, which began to rise again in the 1980s after having declined throughout the 1970s (Bowen and Sosa, 1989).

The situation appears to have changed dramatically since we entered the 1990s. The budgetary crisis we are facing at both federal and state levels has limited the resources available to both the higher education and the research enterprise. Industry, in the face of competitive pressures internationally, has been downsizing, thus further reducing job opportunities. The turmoil accompanying the dramatic revolution that has occurred in Eastern Europe has produced a new source of scientific talent. The U.S. economy has been growing at below average rates, further limiting job creation potential. These events have contributed to the apparent weakness in opportunities that is currently being experienced by new American doctorates. There now seems to be an abundance of applicants for domestic job openings.[4]

In Chapter 6 above, Smith and Tang report that the proportion of new Ph.D.'s who are taking postdoctoral appointments has been high or rising in most fields (NRC, 1993b). This pattern could be reflecting the increasing complexity of the knowledge base in these fields, with a concurrent increase in the need for further training beyond the doctorate. Alternatively, it could be the result of the poor state of the recent job market, in which these temporary appointments are accepted as an interim solution until better permanent opportunities can be found.

Smith and Tang also find, as mentioned above, that an increasing fraction of new doctorates are accepting jobs in industry. This may represent a pull for physical and life scientists and engineers arising from increasing industrial R&D activity. It can also represent a push in the social sciences arising from a lack of sufficient job opportunities in academia, the major employer of Ph.D.'s in this field.

After weighing all of this evidence, I conclude that the labor market for Ph.D. scientists and engineers in the 1980s was moving away from a state of ease, particularly in quantitative fields, although it had not yet reached a state of stringency. As noted earlier, this analysis suggests that, at least in some fields, there may have already existed a pool of scientists who could partially meet future faculty needs.[5] And casual observation of the situation in the early 1990s suggests that demand is weakening again, in part because of the budget problems now being confronted by most academic institutions, in part because of the economic slowdown currently being experienced, and in part because of the pressures on industrial firms to reduce their work forces in order to improve their competitiveness in international markets.

Even if the numbers of people trained and jobs available prove adequate, there remain issues of distribution and competency. Concerns are currently being raised, for example, about the effectiveness of undergraduate teaching—especially in science and engineering fields (U.S. Congress, 1988; Tobias, 1992; Bruffee, 1992). A substantial amount of this teaching is done by graduate students who are teaching assistants. Questions are being raised about the current faculty reward system, which is alleged to favor research over teaching.

Projecting the Future

Exactly what does the future hold? Attempts to forecast future labor market conditions must be accompanied by strong caveats describing their limitations. The accuracy of such forecasts is influenced by the validity of their underlying assumptions about future supply and demand. We cannot anticipate this future with complete accuracy. Moreover, we are plagued by imprecision in our data. Consequently we are also limited in our ability to estimate the exact magnitudes of past relationships used to project supply and demand into the future. All of this produces uncertainty. And it is this uncertainty that must be stressed by producers and kept in mind by consumers of such forecasts (U.S. Congress, Office of Technology Assessment, 1988).

An interesting illustration of the consequences of failure to acknowledge this uncertainty was the estimated future "shortfall" of almost 700,000 bachelor's degrees in the natural sciences and engineering reported by NSF in the mid- and late-1980s (NSF, 1989, 1990c). The results of this analysis were circulated widely. Failure to acknowledge and recognize the conditional nature of the projected shortfalls and the subtle distinctions made by NSF between "shortfalls" and "shortages" led to use of its estimates as justification for initiatives to increase the supply of new graduates. An analysis of the limitations for policymaking of the NSF analysis (Fechter, 1990) led to a serious questioning of both the motives of NSF in circulating such estimates and the validity of any efforts to project future supply and demand (see, e.g., U.S. Congress, 1992).

The literature on future academic labor markets is substantial. It includes the work of Cartter (1976), Freeman (1971, 1976), Radner and Miller (1975), Radner and Kuh (1978), the National Research Council (1979), the National Science Foundation (1979, 1990c), Bowen and Schuster (1986), and, among the most recent, Bowen and Sosa (1989). I focus on the last study, not only because it is the most recent, but because it provides the most field detail and is most explicit about its assumptions and methods.

The literature on the labor market for doctorates is less robust. It includes a series of publications produced by the National Science Foundation that covers scientists and engineers (NSF, 1979), the work of Freeman (1971), and studies of particular fields (Freeman, 1976; Hansen et al., 1980; Baker, 1989, 1991). Many of these studies were undertaken in the 1970s and little attention has been given to this subject since 1980. I focus, therefore, on the most recent efforts: those of Bowen and Sosa and those of the National Science Foundation, efforts which provide a current assessment of future market conditions and which cover a comprehensive set of science fields.

The Bowen and Sosa Model of Ph.D. Faculty

The Bowen and Sosa study limits itself to fields that comprise the arts and sciences—mathematics, physical sciences, psychology, life sciences, humanities, and social sciences. It does not consider fields in which professional practice degrees are granted. Thus, it excludes engineering and the medically oriented fields.

Demand

Future demand is assessed based on anticipated academic job openings. These openings can arise from the need to replace faculty members who leave academia for jobs in other sectors or who retire or die and from the need to create new positions because of growth in faculty employment.

Replacement demand includes two components. The first component— separations for reasons other than death and retirement, or "quits"—is estimated as net outflows from academia. Given lack of adequate data, Bowen and Sosa assume two sets of quit rates: a "high" rate and a "standard" rate.[6] The second component, deaths and retirements, is estimated based on data from two sources. Age-specific retirement rates are based heavily on an American Association of Universities survey of faculty at twelve private universities, the only available source that describes retirement behavior of faculty by age. Mortality rates are derived from the TIAA-CREF insurance program, a program that almost exclusively covers academic employees, both faculty and nonfaculty. Based on these two components of replacement demand, Bowen and Sosa estimate overall "exit probabilities"—that is, the probability that a typical faculty member will not appear in the appropriate faculty age cohort in the next period of their analysis.[7]

Job openings also arise from growth in demand. These are generated based on trends in enrollments in institutions of higher education, the field distribution of those enrollments, and student-faculty ratios. Bowen and Sosa project enrollments by assuming that the enrollment rates that prevailed in 1985 will remain constant at these levels throughout the period of their projections.[8] Based on this assumption, they produce a long-range future enrollment trajectory that is remarkably flat, with smaller cyclical swings than were experienced in earlier periods.

They generate enrollment projections by field using alternative assumptions about future trends in the field distribution of enrollments: (1) that the trends in enrollment shares by field will continue, but at slower rates; (2) that these shares will stabilize at 1984–85 levels; and (3) that these trends will reverse themselves in 1984–85. With the exception of mathematics and physical sciences, which were experiencing a relatively stable share of enrollments, the shares have been declining in each of the fields examined. Thus, one could characterize the first of their assumptions as the most pessimistic with respect to future faculty demand, and one could characterize the third assumption as the most optimistic.

These enrollment projections are converted into faculty demand by means of the student-faculty ratio. Using three alternative estimates of this ratio, Bowen and Sosa consistently find a declining trend for the period 1977–87. This trend suggests that institutions have not been adjusting their faculty demand proportionately to the changes in enrollment they have been experiencing. Possible reasons for this behavior include: (1) a desire on the part of these institutions to minimize staff instability or to maintain minimum staff levels, and (2) increasing demand for faculty in nonteaching functions.

Bowen and Sosa make three assumptions about future values of the student-faculty ratio: (1) that they will remain stable at their 1987 levels; (2) that they will continue their downward trend, but at a progressively slower rate, until 1997, when they will level off; and (3) that they will rise by 5 percent between 1992 and 1997, by 2.5 percent between 1997 and 2002, and will remain constant at 2002 levels thereafter.

Given the assumed scenarios outlined above, there are nine possible alternative models. Bowen and Sosa use four basic models to project net new faculty positions: (1) continuing declines in enrollment shares and stable student-faculty openings; (2) stable enrollment shares and student-faculty ratios; (3) stable enrollment shares and declining student-faculty ratios; and (4) increasing enrollment shares and increasing student-faculty ratios.

Based on these assumptions, Bowen and Sosa report the following findings. Job openings are expected to grow from a range of 19–28,000 in 1987–92 to a range of 33–36,000 in 2007–12. The range of projected increases is considerable, extending from a low of slightly more than 7,000 (26 percent) to a high of 14,000 (76 percent).[9]

Supply

On the supply side of this market, Bowen and Sosa concentrate on the production of new Ph.D.'s, although they recognize that this is not the only source of supply. Bowen and Sosa acknowledge the volatility that has existed in the production of new Ph.D.'s since 1958 and the increasing importance of students on temporary visa status as a component of this production in certain fields. They make two assumptions in projecting supply: (1) that the number of new doctorates who are U.S. residents (which includes U.S. citizens and noncitizens who are permanent residents) will remain stable; and (2) the number of new Ph.D.'s who are nonresidents will increase slightly to 1992, after which it will stabilize at 1992 levels.

To project the supply of new Ph.D.'s to academic institutions, they make two further assumptions about the fraction of new Ph.D.'s who will seek academic positions: (1) that this fraction will remain stable at 1987 levels; and (2) that this share will continue to decline, but at slower rates than were experienced over the past decade. Given these assumptions, the supply of new Ph.D.'s in all arts and science fields is projected to remain reasonably stable at slightly more than 33,000 from the period 1987–92 and thereafter.

Bowen and Sosa compare their alternative projections of total demand with their alternative estimates of supply. In three of the four models they find an excess supply for the five-year intervals 1987–92 and 1992–97 and an excess demand thereafter. Figure 7.1 displays the generic pattern, based on the assumptions embodied in their model 2.

Evaluation of the Model

In evaluating these projections, we must keep in mind that they are based on the particular set of assumptions about demand and supply outlined above. Bowen and Sosa are acutely aware of this. They make no claims for the superiority of their assumptions, and they explicitly acknowledge that others could be valid. To their credit, Bowen and Sosa test the sensitivity of their findings by experimenting with a large number of alternative assumptions. They report that their findings are insensitive to the wide range of alternative scenarios they considered.

While ambitious, however, their sensitivity analysis was not exhaustive. For example, Bowen and Sosa undertook a limited analysis of the sensitivity of the supply/demand ratio to alternative assumptions about the student-faculty ratio. They examine only one scenario in which this ratio is assumed to increase in the future—the scenario in which enroll-

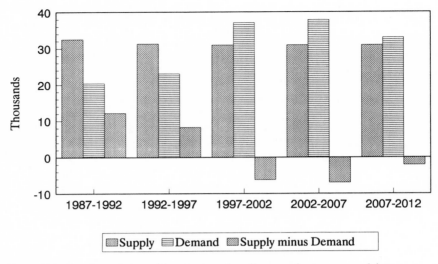

Figure 7.1. Supply and demand projections for all arts and sciences, model 2.

Source: Bowen and Sosa, 1989, p. 128.

ment shares are also assumed to increase in the future. Using their sensitivity analysis, I crudely attempted to determine what might happen to the findings if student-faculty ratios were assumed to increase in other scenarios.

Bowen and Sosa find that varying the assumption about student-faculty ratios reduces faculty demand by about 8,000 in 1997 and by about 13,000 in 2002 and thereafter. The demand reduction is estimated for the model that assumes a stable enrollment share. If this reduction is used to adjust the differences between supply and demand estimated for their model 2 (i.e., stable enrollment shares and stable student-faculty ratios), the excess demand projected for 1997 and beyond is almost entirely eliminated.[10] Like Bowen and Sosa, I do not mean to imply that one scenario is more credible than another; rather, I wish to emphasize that the outcome of this type of analysis is highly sensitive to assumed parameter values and, as a result, there is a great deal of uncertainty associated with the conclusions that can be drawn from it.

An additional feature of the model is that it assumes faculty demand to be solely a function of enrollment; demand arising from research activity is not considered. This could result in an understatement of projected demand trends, especially among the natural science fields and particularly in the research universities. Offsetting this bias, however, is the existence of a large cadre of researchers on postdoctoral and other non–tenure-track research appointments in our major research institutions. These scholars can be an immediate source of supply for future faculty positions.

The National Science Foundation Model of Ph.D.'s

The National Science Foundation has also attempted to assess future market conditions. It confines its analysis to natural science and engineering fields, but it covers nonacademic as well as academic sectors of the economy for the period 1988–2006.

Demand

The demand model is similar to the one employed by Bowen and Sosa. It estimates job openings as the sum of replacement demand and increases in newly created positions. Replacement demand is generated from the age distribution of the Ph.D. work force and age-specific retirement and mortality probabilities of this work force.[11] Like the Bowen and Sosa models, the NSF model projects a rising annual number of replacements in each of the three sectors of the economy, with a doubling from 5,000 to 10,000 to occur by the year 2006.[12]

Sector-specific new-position demand is projected from past statistical relationships between growth in real research spending and growth in Ph.D. employment.[13] Projections are generated from the following assumed real annual growth in rates: industry, 4 percent; academia, 3 percent; other sectors, 1 percent. New-position demand is projected to almost double in industry and academia, rising from approximately 6,600 in 1989 to roughly 12,400 in 2006.[14]

When the projections for these two sources of job openings are combined, the number of openings in industry and academia is expected to almost double by the year 2006, rising from about 12,000 to roughly 23,000. The number of job openings in other sectors is also projected to grow by a small but unspecified amount.

Supply

The supply model is also similar in its general structure to the Bowen and Sosa model in its distinction between native-born and foreign-born doctorates. It assumes that the annual number of foreign-born doctorates will remain unchanged at 4,500, slightly above the 1988 level.[15]

The model departs from the Bowen-Sosa approach by linking production of native-born doctorates to past production of bachelor's degrees in natural science and engineering fields. Specifically, it assumes that field-specific "continuation rates" will remain fixed at current levels. Thus, future changes in Ph.D. production will occur from changes in lagged production of bachelor's degrees in natural science and engineering fields[16] and from changes in the doctoral field distribution of these baccalaureates.

Given these assumptions, the model projects that Ph.D. production in natural science and engineering fields will rise slightly between 1988 and 1993, from 14,600 to 15,800. It then projects a more dramatic decline to a range of 13,000–14,000 in 1996 through the first decade of the next century (NSF, 1990c, p. 15).

Based on the assumptions and numbers described above, the model concludes that by the year 2006 the annual number of job openings will exceed the annual number of new degrees produced by roughly 9,000. This reinforces the Bowen-Sosa conclusion that the market for academics in natural sciences is likely to become more stringent for employers as we approach the turn of the century.

Evaluation of the Model

Unfortunately, the projections generated by this model are subject to only minimal effort to determine the sensitivity of the results to alternative assumptions. Specifically, projections of supply are generated assuming these conditions: (1) no changes in real salaries of doctorates, and (2) changes in real salaries that will exhaust the projected salary portion of the teaching and research budget.[17] Projections generated by this model have figured prominently in recommendations for increases in student support (see, e.g., Atkinson, 1990).

Policy Implications

These models share a characteristic that biases them in the direction of overstating supply/demand imbalances; they do not include any market feedback mechanisms. In simple terms, this means that the models assume that supply does not respond to shifts in demand and vice versa. The assumption that feedback does not occur thus makes projections generated by such models worst-case scenarios.[18]

Acknowledging the existence of such mechanisms transforms the issue at hand from whether there will be enough or too many Ph.D. scientists and engineers to the types of adjustments that can be expected to occur in the absence of policy intervention and the expected speed with which these adjustments can be expected to eliminate market imbalances. For example, to reduce excess demand, academic administrators may allow student-faculty ratios to rise. Such a decision will have an immediate impact, but policymakers may wish to ask whether such increases will be socially desirable. The answer is not immediately evident. Increases in the ratio can alleviate pressure on tuition by reducing the average cost of the teaching input. But heavier teaching loads could act as a deterrent to effective recruiting.[19] An increased student-faculty ratio may also affect the quality of the product. Larger classes are not generally perceived to be a move in the direction of higher quality higher education, although research does not strongly support this case.

A similar but more general argument can be made for the use of increased wages for equilibrating supply and demand—the "free market" solution. Such increases can be expected to reduce the supply-demand imbalance (by providing incentives to students to acquire degrees in these fields, thereby increasing the supply of new Ph.D.'s). Most employers are constrained in the amount of discretion they possess in the salary setting process. Thus, wage adjustments will not occur instantaneously. And, in some circumstances, significant nonwage adjustments may occur. Moreover, given the extensive amount of time required to complete doctorate training, the impact of salary changes can be expected to occur with a further lag.

As noted earlier, the National Science Foundation examines the sensitivity of their findings to one particular mechanism: an increase in real salaries. They find that research and teaching will become more expensive, a larger number of Ph.D.'s will be granted, and the projected growth rates in real research spending will not be supportable.

Employers can also change their standards for hiring. For example, during periods of shortages they can hire candidates who have not completed their doctoral requirements. This happened in the 1960s, a period of dramatic growth in demand for scientists. During periods of plentiful supply they can limit their hiring to candidates who have completed their doctoral work and who have received their degrees from one of the top-ranked universities. We saw this phenomenon at work during the 1970s when the market for scientists was relatively stagnant. Academic administrators and faculty can also take actions that reduce the amount of time it takes to complete the doctorate or can shift resources from postdoctoral appointments to faculty appointments.

One can argue that each of the examples discussed above will operate to increase costs or to reduce quality. One can make similar arguments for each of the other equilibrating mechanisms that can be used. Knowledge about what determines the choice of mechanisms and the impact these choices have on supply and demand in both quantitative and qualitative terms would, therefore, be quite useful. The literature on these issues is not extensive and the small amount that exists is not very current.[20] Clearly, they merit further inquiry.

One can gain some insight, however, through speculation. It seems reasonable to assume that the choice of mechanisms will depend significantly on the expected permanence of the changes that gave rise to the market imbalances. Permanent changes can be expected to lead to the adoption of measures that will be enduring in their impact. For example, in academia, changes in student-faculty ratios or in the use of part-time or non–tenure-track faculty appointees are more flexible as adjustment mechanisms than are changes in faculty salaries. Thus, one would expect the use of the former mechanisms when imbalances are perceived to be temporary and the use of the latter when imbalances are expected to be more long run in their duration.

Given the assumptions of the Bowen-Sosa and the NSF models, one would expect an increase in job openings beginning in the latter part of the 1990s. In the case of the Bowen-Sosa model, this increase will last until at least 2012, a period of at least fifteen years. Thus, if a situation of shortage develops, it undoubtedly will not be expected to be a transitory phenomenon, and decision makers in this market will be inclined to adopt remedies that will be enduring in their impact.

Given these expectations, it would be reasonable to expect real salaries to rise, providing more incentive to students to choose careers in these fields and giving greater motivation to employers to adopt measures that will make more efficient use of this more expensive resource. We may already be seeing the effects of the recruiting difficulties of the 1980s on student choices. The proportion of college freshmen interested in obtaining doctoral degrees and the number of domestic students acquiring doctorates in the natural sciences has been increasing in recent years (Astin et al., 1993).

Obviously, expectations about market conditions may not be the only factor associated with this recent trend. Programs providing support for graduate study have also been growing and the pool from which new doctorates are drawn, bachelor's degree recipients from earlier periods, expanded rapidly in the early and mid-1980s. This pool has been declining in more recent years.

Given lags in supply response, however, employers may also have to use short-term mechanisms to meet their immediate needs. Thus, one might also expect to observe increases in student/faculty ratios, greater reliance on part-time and non–tenure-track faculty, and some relaxation in hiring standards.

As noted earlier in this chapter, however, there are already forces at work that have generated increases in supply and decreases in demand, and these forces must be taken into account in formulating future policy. Under these circumstances, one might be tempted to ask whether any intervention will be necessary. Given the range of uncertainty associated with the projected outcomes and given the bias toward overstatement of projected market imbalances that is embedded in the typical projection model, any actions contemplated should not have as their objective the elimination of projected imbalances. Both studies caution that their projections should not be taken too literally.

The range of uncertainty associated with these projections and recent changes in supply and demand suggest that there may not be any significant shortages—that "market forces" will ultimately operate to eliminate them. Indeed, we may be confronted with an overabundance of talent as we enter the next century. While there is no doubt that market forces will ultimately operate, it is not clear they will operate quickly enough, given the long lags and the administrative constraints associated with this particular labor market.

Moreover, some adjustments may have undesirable impacts. For example, market-generated increases in salaries may result in tuition increases or increases in the cost of conducting research. Such impacts may be considered undesirable because they make access to higher education more difficult and they make research effort more expensive. An alternative mechanism, one which is manipulable by policy, would be increased graduate student support. Such a policy would expand supply without raising salaries, thus minimizing possible adverse effects on tuition and costs.

Given these biases and uncertainties, policymakers might wish to adopt a strategy that minimizes the cost of an incorrect decision. One can incorrectly assume that intervention will be necessary; or one can erroneously assume that intervention will not be necessary. The cost of the former decision could be some excess supply of Ph.D. scientists in the future. The cost of the latter decision could be some combination of excess demand and other adverse impacts, such as quality deterioration in teaching and research or undesirable increases in tuition costs.

My personal preference would be for the former strategy—that is, to assume intervention will be necessary. I would not, however, focus on a particular support mechanism, such as fellowships, in formulating this policy. Instead, I would consider the total range of support mechanisms—fellowships, traineeships, research assistantships, and teaching assistantships. The history of student support since 1975 shows that it has been increasing by almost 2 percent per year, spurred largely by increases in teaching and research assistantships that have more than offset declines in fellowships and traineeships.[21] Under these conditions, policy formulation based solely on what has been happening to fellowships would produce inappropriate recommendations.

The recommendations that flow from the National Science Foundation study are a case in point. Recall that this study projects a shortage of roughly 9,000 new doctorates in natural science and engineering fields. Based on this finding, Atkinson recommended an increase of roughly 9,000 in the number of fellowships that should be provided. But further recall that, in the NSF model, demand was partially based on growth in real research spending. If one assumes that such spending is also used to support graduate students (in the form of research assistantships), then 9,000 overstates the number of fellowships needed to eliminate the gap.

Some policy issues may be independent of the current or projected state of the labor market. A notable example is underrepresented groups—women and members of underrepresented racial/ethnic groups—an issue receiving much attention in this volume. Underrepresentation in part reflects barriers that prevent qualified individuals from these groups from pursuing scientific careers. Therefore, underrepresentation is an indicator of talent that is not exploited to its fullest potential. Such underutilization, which can exist simultaneously with situations of abundance, represents a cost to society as well as to the individuals in these groups. And policy formulation aimed at reducing this underrepresentation should not be totally based on market conditions.

Finally, I would closely monitor actual experience compared with what models such as those summarized in this chapter project. Such monitorship will enable us to make midcourse corrections in projections, if such corrections are deemed necessary. Policy measures could then be reassessed and modified accordingly.

Proper tracking and monitoring of these models raises further issues. What should be the criteria for evaluation and midcourse corrections? Will these adjustments be made quickly enough to permit changes in policy? These issues lie beyond the scope of this study. But, surely, they must be addressed to make modelling efforts such as these more meaningful for policy formulation.

Notes

1. Tuckman et al., 1993. The estimate is based on total (rather than registered) time since receipt of the bachelor's degree.

2. See Leslie and Oaxaca (1993) for a recent review of the performance of such efforts. Notable exceptions include the works of Allan Cartter (1976), who projected the reversal of the trend in academic demand that occurred in the late 1960s and early 1980s, and DauffenBach and Fiorito (1983), who concluded that the defense buildup of the late 1970s and early 1980s would not cause serious bottlenecks.

See also National Research Council (1986) for a study that supported the Dauffen-Bach and Fiorito conclusions.

3. See also Chapter 6 above for a more detailed discussion of foreign doctorates.

4. David Goodstein, in several provocative articles (1993a, 1993b), suggests that the current situation is a manifestation of a more fundamental phenomenon: an end to the centuries of exponential growth experienced by the scientific enterprise since about 1700. He argues, therefore, that the current weaknesses in scientific labor markets are not transitory and will not eventually vanish with renewed growth.

5. Postdocs, those in academia in non–tenure-track positions, and those employed in industry because of lack of job opportunities in academia are potential sources of supply.

6. The "high" rate assumes a quit rate of 1 percent per year for tenured faculty and 10 percent per year for nontenured faculty. The "standard" rate assumes rates of 0.5 percent per year and 5 percent per year for tenured and nontenured faculty, respectively. These rates are applied to within–age group distributions of faculty by tenure status to derive age-specific quit rates.

7. They use five-year intervals for both their age cohorts and their periods of analysis.

8. The enrollment rate is the number enrolled in institutions of higher education divided by the number in the population of potential enrollees. Bowen and Sosa calculate these rates for specific age cohorts.

9. The results are largely driven by the reversal in trend for total enrollments projected for 1997. Net new faculty demand is either negative or trivially positive prior to 1997. This demand becomes strongly positive for the period 1997–2007, after which it becomes trivially positive again for the period 2007–12.

10. I hasten to point out, however, that Bowen and Sosa would consider this outcome inadequate. Based in part on historical experience, they argue that a supply-demand ratio of approximately 1.3 seems closer to the norm than a ratio of 1.0. They argue that a ratio that is greater than 1.0 is the appropriate target to achieve because of frictional forces that occur in all labor markets. They contend that these forces are especially serious in academic markets because of the relatively high degree of specialization required for any particular academic position; Bowen and Sosa (1989, pp. 166–71) and unpublished correspondence from William G. Bowen dated April 5, 1990.

11. NSF, 1990c, p. 16. Unfortunately, the detailed methodology used to generate the number of replacements is not described.

12. Smaller numbers are projected for replacement demand in earlier years: 6,000 in the mid-1990s and 8,000 at the turn of the century.

13. NSF, 1990c, p. 17. The relationship between changes in enrollment and changes in Ph.D. employment is also utilized in projecting academic employment. Unfortunately, no information is provided to describe the method used to estimate these relationships or the magnitude of the relationships generated from this analysis.

14. These projected rates assume a continuation of the averages that prevailed over the past twenty years. I presume this covers the period 1968–87.

15. This number is the product of two factors: (1) the number of foreign citizens on student visas receiving doctorate in natural science and engineering fields and (2) the fraction of those doctorates who remain in the United States.

16. The period of the lag is not explicitly described; based on material in the text, I assume it is either six or seven years.

17. NSF, 1990c, 20. Projections of this budget appear to be based on a model of Ph.D. labor markets which assumes that demand is relatively insensitive to changes in real salaries (a 1 percent change in these salaries produces a less than 1 percent change in employment), that native-born supply is moderately sensitive to changes in real salaries (a 1 percent change in salaries produces an approximately 1 percent change in Ph.D production), and that foreign supply is quite sensitive to changes in real salaries (a 1 percent change in salaries produces a 1.5 percent change in Ph.D. production). Unfortunately, neither the labor market model nor the model linking the parameters of this model to the salary costs of teaching and research are described in detail.

18. The modelers recognize this limitation and devote effort to discussing the implications of various types of mechanisms. See, e.g., Bowen and Sosa, 1989, 144–71; and NSF, 1990c, pp. 18–21.

19. See Bowen and Sosa (1989, p. 151) for a cogent statement of this argument.

20. For a thorough review of the literature, see Ehrenberg (1991).

21. The number of full-time science and engineering graduate students supported by fellowships and traineeships rose by roughly 1 percent from 30,900 in 1980 to 31,200 in 1989; the number supported by research and teaching assistantships rose by 30 percent from 99,200 to 130,200 (see NSB, 1991, table 2-17, p. 229).

CHAPTER 8

Human Resources in Science and Engineering: Policy Implications

Cheryl B. Leggon and Shirley M. Malcom

In other chapters of this volume, Betty Vetter, Terrence Russell, and Earl Smith and Joyce Tang systematically examine the flow of student talent through the higher education science and engineering (S/E) pipeline and, ultimately, to the workplace. The common theme that runs through these chapters is the dramatic underrepresentation of women and non-Asian minorities in these careers. In his analysis of prospective supply and demand for Ph.D.'s, Alan Fechter contends that such forecasts are associated with a great deal of uncertainty. Fechter notes that the two models used most frequently to forecast supply and demand for S/E workers in the United States—the National Science Foundation's (NSF) model for doctorates in the natural sciences and engineering, and the Bowen and Sosa model for arts and sciences faculty—substantially overstate expected shortages. Science policy analysts and scientists and engineers themselves disagree about the magnitude of the projected shortages, about whether there will be any shortages, and if so, about what they will mean for the United States. Some observers, such as University of California at San Diego Chancellor Richard Atkinson (1990), see the projected S/E shortages as detrimental to the S/E enterprise because they will put the United States at a competitive disadvantage in world markets. Others, such as economists Sharon Levin and Paula Stephan (1991), see them as beneficial because they decrease the numbers of scientists competing for basic research grants. This competition is becoming increasingly fierce as cutbacks in state funding to public and private academic institutions compel researchers to seek more federal grant support (Twombly, 1992).

Although the debate concerning the adequacy of the U.S. human resource base to meet its future needs for S/E talent has focused on projected shortages of scientists and engineers, we argue that regardless of whether these shortages materialize, it is necessary for the United States to expand the pool from which S/E talent is recruited. In our opinion, the problem is *not* one of supply but of distribution—that is, the ability of the current system to respond to the need to diversify the current S/E talent pool. Increasing the participation of non-Asian minorities in S/E careers is a desirable policy objective *not* only to meet some moral or ethical imperative, nor even to meet projected shortages, but to enrich the entire S/E enterprise. The underrepresentation commonly found in the chapters by Vetter, Russell, and Smith and Tang strongly suggests underemployment and underutilization of the significant talent pools that are growing and are expected to become even more important sources of talent for our country in the future.

Thus, diversity of the S/E talent pool is a significant issue—whether or not projected shortages materialize (U.S. Congress, 1991). Market forces alone cannot increase the diversity of the S/E workforce. We address in this chapter the question of how to increase the diversity of the S/E talent pool to include those who are projected by the year 2000 to be the majority of the overall U.S. work force: women and non-Asian minorities.

Meeting the Need: Supply Options

The traditional pool of white males has been experiencing declines not only in its proportion of the U.S. population but also in terms of its interest in pursuing S/E careers; this decline in interest has occurred both among the "rank and file" and also among the "best and the brightest"— such as the male National Merit Scholars, for whom interest in science peaked in 1984 (Vetter, Chapter 1 above). What can be done to offset the decline in this traditional source of S/E talent? One way to maintain the current level of degree production in S/E fields is to increase the proportions for all sources of S/E talent.[1]

Short-Term Solutions

The short-term solutions suggested by Russell (Chapter 5 above) for the field of chemistry may be applicable to other fields. If the B.S. degree is the basic entry-level credential into technical industry jobs in the United States, and we cannot attract more U.S. students to chemistry, then skill requirements must be met in the short term by using workers with technical training that lacks the breadth of a B.S. degree in chemistry. This could produce adverse performance and productivity effects. At the Ph.D. level, an additional short-term source of available S/E talent for faculty positions includes researchers on postdoctoral and other non–tenure-track research appointments.

Another short-term source of Ph.D. talent is non–U.S. citizens. Between 1969 and 1989, the proportion of doctorates earned by non–U.S.

citizens more than doubled in the physical sciences (from 16 percent to 36 percent) and in engineering (from 25 percent to 55 percent).[2] Anecdotal data suggest that cultural differences between foreign-born faculty and U.S.–born students might discourage U.S. students from majoring in science or engineering; this could be even worse for female and minority male students (NRC, 1988, 21). Thus, using foreign-born doctorates to meet projected S/E faculty shortages in the United States may be a short-term solution with potentially negative consequences for long-term supply of S/E talent. In addition, because the long-term availability of foreign-born doctorates is unpredictable, they provide an unstable source of S/E talent for the United States.

Long-Term Solutions

Efforts to increase the proportion of students entering S/E careers by increasing their interest in S/E fields is a long-term solution because of the amount of time required to educate and train for these careers. As noted earlier, there is a common theme of underrepresentation of women and non-Asian minorities throughout this volume.

Women

Women comprise slightly more than 50 percent of the total U.S. population, 45 percent of total employment, 50 percent of employment in professional and related populations, but only about 33 percent of the scientists—including social and behavioral scientists—and only 4 percent of the engineers (NSF, 1990d). Not only do women comprise more than half of U.S. high school graduates, but females of every racial and ethnic group are more likely than males to graduate from high school (Vetter, 1989). Although women comprise more than half of the undergraduate enrollments, they comprise less than half of the graduate enrollments and continue to underparticipate in all fields of natural science and engineering, even at the bachelor's level.[3]

Vetter (Chapter 1 above) and Etzkowitz et al. (Chapter 3 above) contend that women are progressively alienated from science. One of the main forces working against women's participation in science is a masculine image of the scientific role that has already taken hold by primary school and that deters women from taking mathematics in secondary school (Etzkowitz et al., Chapter 3). At the elementary and secondary levels, gender differences in science achievement are predominantly due to the accumulated effects of sex-role stereotypes in family, school, and society. For example, most American parents accept the myth that their daughters—solely because of their sex—are less talented in mechanics and mathematics than their sons (Vetter, Chapter 1). This belief then sets in motion a self-confirming stereotype in which girls are not exposed to mathematics and mechanics because they are believed not to be talented in them, and they later cannot become talented because they were not exposed to them earlier.[4]

After receiving their bachelor's degrees and during graduate school, women drop out of graduate school more frequently than men. This difference is attributable to two sets of factors, according to Etzkowitz et al. (Chapter 3). The first set of factors, cumulative disadvantage, stems from the different ways in which males and females are socialized. For example, girls are socialized to seek help rather than to be self-reliant or to function autonomously or competitively, like boys. Changes in socialization practices can channel women's interest in S/E careers.

Although they may be able to do little about the first set of factors resulting in cumulative disadvantages, graduate departments *can* do something about the second set that result in "marginal disadvantage." Marginal disadvantages are reflected in recruitment and retention practices, advisement, role modeling, and hiring practices that either discourage women or place them at a competitively inferior position when compared to men. Graduate departments can develop and implement activities focusing on recruitment and retention; the WEPAN survey found that between 1982 and 1987, the decline in such activities paralleled the decline in the number of women enrolling in engineering (Matyas, Chapter 2 above).

A major factor hampering the impact of S/E intervention efforts in the United States is the limited number and the maldistribution of programs targeting women (Matyas, Chapter 2). Given their high school graduation rates and undergraduate enrollments, women represent a promising source of additional S/E talent. Universities can revise the academic structure to eliminate the gender-related obstacles to entry or retention highlighted in Etzkowitz et al.[5]

Non-Asian Minorities

By the year 2000, one in every three American students will be a member of a racial or ethnic minority; currently, twenty-two of the twenty-five largest school districts in the United States have a predominantly minority enrollment (Quality Education for Minorities Project, 1990, p. 11). Nevertheless, based on their respective proportions of the U.S. population, African Americans and Hispanics participate at lower levels in U.S. graduate and professional schools than do non-Hispanic whites, some Asians, and nonresident aliens. Non-Asian minority groups differ in their high-school graduation rates: Hispanics are less likely to graduate from high school than are either African Americans or non-Hispanic whites. In sum, there are differences among non-Asian minority groups in terms of their rates of high school graduation, undergraduate and graduate enrollments, and participation in S/E careers.

Trent and Hill (Chapter 4) note that historically black colleges and universities (HBCUs) have traditionally played a leading role in the education of African American scientists and engineers. They have done so by providing a nurturing environment that helps students to overcome the obstacles to S/E careers created by inadequate precollege preparation. Given the track record of HBCUs, Hill and Trent suggest that additional resources allocated to them can further increase the number of African Americans who will choose careers in these fields.

Policy Implications

Given the uncertainty of projections, we believe, along with the Office of Technology Assessment (U.S. Congress, 1991), that the most robust policy is to maximize the preparedness of all groups—including white males—in the S/E doctorate pipeline. Within racial/ethnic groups, intragroup differences—based on gender and class—are at least as significant as differences among racial/ethnic groups (Leggon, 1987). Thus, to be effective in meeting the United States's future needs for S/E talent, human resource policy must be informed not only by overall S/E pipeline dynamics (i.e., movement in, through, and out) but also by those dynamics disaggregated by race/ethnicity and gender (Leggon, 1987, 1991a, 1991b).

Targeted Policies and Programs

Costs and benefits will result from the United States acting—or failing to act—to increase the participation of non-Asian minorities in S/E careers. The accuracy of projected S/E shortages can be determined only with hindsight, and even then in a limited way. Therefore, the United States has two choices: do nothing now to increase non-Asian minority participation in S/E careers and "pay later" if the projected shortages materialize; or do something now to increase this participation and have "too many" scientists and engineers, if the projected S/E shortages do not materialize. In our view, the latter choice is preferable for three reasons. First, not only does it broaden and deepen the S/E talent pool, but it also enriches the problems studied and the perspectives brought to bear on the S/E enterprise. Second, if we believe that science and technology enhance society's standard of living, then it is impossible to have "too many" scientists and engineers, because they can contribute to society's welfare by working in government and industry, as well as in basic research. Finally, and perhaps most important, we agree with Leon Lederman's assertion that increased participation in S/E careers will help to cement the national community insofar as it reduces the educational inequalities among groups in the United States (Lederman, 1992).

The Four R's of Policy Intervention

Policies and programs to increase participation in S/E careers by under-participating groups tend to focus on recruitment and retention (U.S. Congress, 1988). To these, we add two more aspects—readiness and revitalization—to describe the full spectrum of issues and policy targets. Our operational definitions of these four R's follow.

Readiness refers to the set of K–12 experiences that permit students to successfully matriculate in college-level science and mathematics courses. *Recruitment* refers to the set of activities that attract students to major in science, engineering, or related fields, or to choose elective courses in science and mathematics. *Retention* refers to the set of actions and programs that seek to interest students in S/E careers, get students to use science in their everyday life, or provide students with a base for lifelong learning in science and related fields. *Revitalization* refers to the process by which students are encouraged and assisted to further study in S/E fields.

Federal support of S/E intervention programs affects both retention and revitalization by further training qualified S/E students who, as they apprentice in the research community, are able to add their perspectives to the knowledge base through their choices of problems and perspectives, both of which are influenced by the experiences that they bring.

The Three Stages of S/E Intervention Programs

There are basically three stages in the sociohistorical development of federally funded S/E intervention programs in the United States. The first stage, which encompassed the years from 1957 through 1969, we call the "pre-equity stage" because its programs did not target any particular group and were spinoffs from the post-Sputnik programs of general science education reform. Following the former Soviet Union's launch of Sputnik, the United States declared itself to be in a "crisis" in science education. One response to this crisis was to create federal programs focusing on science and engineering at several different levels of the pipeline. For example, concerns about the quality of precollegiate preparation in science and mathematics prompted the formulation of big projects to develop quality curricula in the various fields of science and a massive effort to retrain teachers. In addition, many programs have provided support for graduate- and postdoctoral-level training.

What effect did these efforts have on minorities and women in terms of degree attainment and career participation in science and engineering? During the late 1960s, post-Sputnik science education efforts were designed to attract *all* Americans to S/E careers. These efforts may have resulted in some benefits to underparticipating groups, such as increased opportunities to pursue S/E careers; however, these benefits were incidental and can be characterized as spillovers from the larger effort to recruit and train the traditional sources of talent.

The second stage began in 1970 and marked a shift from nontargeted programs to specific interventions at different parts of the educational pipeline; particular attention was given to those parts that were untouched by any programs for many years—such as, for example, pre–high school. The earliest efforts to target specifically underparticipating groups date from the late 1960s and early 1970s, when policy responses to African Americans' civil rights demands were translated into programs. Some efforts were targeted to provide science resources in HBCUs, such as the 1972 formation of COSIP-D (a targeted component of the larger College Science Improvement Program of the National Science Foundation). Professional societies soon followed suit. For example, in 1968, the American Chemical Society (ACS) established Project SEED to provide disadvantaged youth with a summer experience in a chemistry laboratory. Within the American Association for the Advancement of Science (AAAS), ad hoc committees for women and minorities began forming in the late 1960s and early 1970s. In 1972, these groups' efforts led to the passage of an equal opportunity resolution, the establishment of a board committee, and the staffing of an office to achieve equal opportunities goals (AAAS, 1992).

As the women's movement grew in momentum and Title IX of the Education Amendments Act of 1972 was passed, programs to address women's participation in science and engineering were established. The targeting of funding toward science and engineering resulted largely from efforts of the Women's Educational Equity Act Program, which focused on nontraditional careers for women. Participants in these S/E programs were also supported by a series of programs within the NSF aimed at career awareness and career exploration for girls and young women, and career reentry for women trained in science whose careers may have been interrupted.

The third stage, which began in 1981, was characterized by a shift in the rationale for intervention efforts from equity issues to demographic issues. Indeed, the federal role in science education was questioned, and the education directorate of the NSF was dissolved. As research supported the argument that the role of white males in the U.S. work force in general and in the S/E work force in particular was diminishing, the importance of women and minorities in both work forces increased. Consequently, federally funded programs focused on underparticipating groups.

This focus was concentrated on programs for minorities. According to the AAAS Office of Opportunities in Sciences 1983 survey, over half of all the programs responding were targeted to minority students or faculty; less than 10 percent of the programs were targeted to women (Malcom,

1984). This differential targeting may have resulted from trends indicating that women were moving into S/E fields, as a result of stage 1 programs; these trends may have led to the belief that at least women's problems were solved (or would eventually solve themselves). The leveling off in the mid-1980s of women's participation in engineering, however, showed that deeper structural problems remain (Matyas and Malcom, 1991).

Although most S/E intervention programs remain demographically driven, we contend that they must move to the next stage, in which total participation in science and engineering is increased by addressing the opportunities and motivation of presently underparticipating groups. Because the demographic realities that create majority-minority systems defeat intervention-based approaches by the sheer magnitude of populations to be served, we propose that mechanisms for addressing equity issues be embedded throughout the infrastructure of the nation's S/E enterprise. Such programs must also be geographically dispersed. This would be consistent with moving to the next stage in the evolution of intervention programs.

Based on descriptions of intervention programs and case studies, Matyas and Malcom (1991) developed a model for the evolution of intervention programs. This model includes five levels: (1) isolated projects or programs; (2) department- or school-based efforts; (3) formal coordination of discrete projects; (4) centers created for the coordination of large parts of the process of recruiting, retaining, tracking, and advancing students to graduate education; and (5) structural reform where the structure of courses, pedagogical techniques, institutional climate, and system for recruitment and retention coexist with a supportive administrative structure.

Most S/E intervention programs start as a separate set of activities funded by external sources (Matyas, Chapter 2). Matyas and Malcom (1991) found that the intervention efforts of most institutions were at the first level—that is, isolated projects and programs not connected in any way—and relied primarily on soft money for support. Moreover, at all education levels, from precollege through graduate, these programs were less likely to be mainstreamed into departmental or institutional budgets; this means that effective practices from these programs are also less likely to be integrated into institutional programs.

The establishment of the NSF Statewide Systematic Initiatives in Science, Mathematics, and Engineering Program (SSI) is a step that could lead to structurally integrating equity issues in reform. This will be possible, however, only if careful thought is given to integrating equity concerns in the activities, policies, educational programs, and especially the vision that direct such reform. Although it focuses largely on K–12 reform, SSI is based in a systemic perspective that recognizes that K–12 is but a part of the entire system. Consequently, SSI guidelines are flexible enough to allow proposals to address the higher education components of that system. Such flexibility is the most robust policy for improving the preparedness of the S/E pipeline—particularly given the uncertainty of projections (U.S. Congress, 1991; Fechter, Chapter 7 above).

Systematic collection of data, monitoring, and follow-up are characteristics of successful institutional programs. Institutions must collect and disseminate data not only on recruitment but also on retention. Just as some institutions publish the graduation rates of their athletes, so too should they compile, analyze, and disseminate the graduation rates of their students by major field. Recently, the National Action Council for Minorities in Engineering (NACME) compared the success of American engineering schools in graduating minorities—African Americans, Hispanics, and Native Americans (NACME, 1991). NACME operationalized this success in terms of three parameters: the absolute number of graduates, the graduation rates of minorities, and the Relative Retention Index (RRI)—that is, the graduation rates of minorities relative to those of nonminorities (NACME, 1991). In our opinion, retention rates by major field and education institution data should also be collected and analyzed on an ongoing basis by organizations such as the National Research Council or the National Science Foundation.

Retention data provide three major benefits. First, they enable students to make better informed decisions about which higher education institution to attend. Second, they provide feedback for institutions to identify those elements that facilitate and impede retention, and to make the requisite corrections to their policies, programs, and practices. Third, they enhance the process by which institutions are held accountable, by identifying both successful and unsuccessful S/E intervention programs so that they may be rewarded—or not—accordingly. Most intervention programs have *not* been evaluated extensively (Matyas, Chapter 2). Sponsors must build into S/E intervention programs both the requirement that they be evaluated and the funds to do so.

Over the years while attempting to build an infrastructure to support S/E participation by underparticipating groups, researchers, advocates, and policymakers have debated the best ways to proceed toward reform. Should S/E intervention programs focus on the individual or the institution? Should these programs be targeted or mainstreamed? Should they take the project or systemic approach? Human resource policy in science and engineering should also focus on the organizational issues that institutions must address (Matyas, Chapter 2; see also Tobias, 1992; and NRC, 1991b). For example, since research indicates that faculty participation in S/E intervention programs is a crucial ingredient in program success, colleges and universities should count this participation in the tenure process

(Matyas, Chapter 2); this would make faculty participation in these programs more consonant with other institutional goals. Another example: both graduate and faculty programs must establish ongoing partnerships with S/E faculty and administrators at higher education institutions that serve large numbers of minority students to develop a pool of minorities for graduate and faculty positions (Trent and Hill, Chapter 4; and Matyas, Chapter 2).

The long-term survival, effectiveness, and success of S/E intervention programs depend on the support and commitment of the host institution and on sustained funding (U.S. Congress, 1991). Program sponsors from the public *and* private sectors should leverage their funds by rewarding those institutions that have an established track record in recruiting and retaining underparticipating groups in science and engineering, and those who want to contribute to the diversity of the pool (Pearson and Bechtel, 1989). For example, federal, state, and private sector S/E organizations could reward HBCUs for their record—especially at the baccalaureate level—of producing African American scientists and engineers; such rewards could include increasing the instructional resources and faculty support available to the HBCUs.

Market forces alone cannot increase the size and diversity of the S/E work force in the United States. Policy intervention will continue to be required to increase the diversity of the S/E work force. To be effective, intervention should be based on a perspective that views the S/E pipeline as a system in which efforts targeted to one part of the system have consequences, unintended as well as intended, for other parts of the system. Successful efforts resulting from such deliberate policy should be rewarded.

Systemic reform need not—perhaps cannot—occur at once, but in bits and pieces that, over time, add up to reform of the entire system. Such incremental reforms must be sufficiently flexible to facilitate making corrections in the system as needed, and should be carefully monitored to ensure that they are consistent with the policy that informs them. One mechanism for this coordinating function at the federal level could be the Office of Science and Technology's Federal Coordinating Council for Science, Engineering, and Technology (FCCSET).[6] Further, coordination between public and private sector players could be facilitated under the auspices of organizations with appropriate ties to the science and engineering community.

In sum, we contend that carefully crafted human resource policy (informed by systematic data collection and analysis) combined with flexible programs and practices will generate the systemic reform necessary to increase the size and diversity of the U.S. S/E work force.

Notes

1. Longitudinal data give apparently conflicting signals: on the one hand, they indicate a lessening interest among all students in selecting a S/E major; on the other, they indicate an increase in the fraction of American freshmen expressing an interest in obtaining a doctoral degree (Astin et al., 1988).

2. This increase is largely attributable to temporary visa holders who earned 9 percent of all U.S. doctorates in 1960, and 21 percent in 1989 (NRC, 1989b).

3. For first-person accounts of barriers presented by undergraduate "gatekeepers" in science courses, see Tobias (1990).

4. On self-confirming stereotypes, see Merton (1973b).

5. For example, departments have prohibitions against hiring their own graduates. These apparently neutral prohibitions have a more negative impact on female scientists and engineers than on their male counterparts. As Etzkowitz et al. (Chapter 3) point out, however, as more male scientists and engineers marry women whose careers are important to them, male geographical mobility will also be slowed. Consequently, if universities relax prohibitions against hiring their own graduates, female scientists and engineers would be as geographically mobile as their male counterparts, and, therefore, have less of a disadvantage in terms of job seeking.

6. The Federal Coordinating Council on Science, Engineering, and Technology (FCCSET) is a standing mechanism consisting of committees and subcommittees that facilitates coordination of research and development activities throughout federal agencies. FCCSET has participated extensively in implementing programs in several presidential priority areas, including global climate change, high-performance computing, and mathematics and science education (U.S. Congress, 1991).

References

Abir-Am, Pnina. 1991. "Science Policy for Women in Science: From Historical Case Studies to an Agenda for the 1990's." Paper presented at the joint meetings of the Society for the History of Technology and History of Science Society, Madison, Wisconsin, November 2.

Abir-Am, Pnina, and Dorinda Outram. 1987. *Uneasy Careers and Intimate Lives.* New Brunswick: Rutgers University Press.

Adams v. Richardson. 1973. 356 F. Supp. 92 (D.C. 1973), modified, 480 F. 2d 1159 (D.C. Cir. 1973).

Adelman, Clifford. 1991. *Women at Thirtysomething: Paradoxes of Attainment.* Washington, D.C.: U.S. Department of Education, Office of Educational Research and Development.

Aldridge, Bill. 1990. "Improving Pre-college Science Education." Pp. 70–75 in Betty M. Vetter, ed., *Human Resources in Science and Technology: Improving U.S. Competitiveness.* Washington, D.C.: Commission on Professionals in Science and Technology.

Allen, Walter, Edgar Epps, and Nesha Haniff. 1991. *College in Black and White.* Albany: State University of New York Press.

American Association for the Advancement of Science (AAAS). 1992. *1992–93 AAAS Handbook of Officers, Organization, Activities.* Washington, D.C.: AAAS.

American Association of Engineering Societies (AAES). 1989. "Women in Engineering." *Engineering Manpower Bulletin* 99 (December): 1–5.

American Association of University Women (AAUW). 1991. *Shortchanging Girls, Shortchanging America.* Washington, D.C.: AAUW. Executive Summary.

———. 1992. *How Schools Shortchange Girls.* Washington, D.C.: AAUW.

American Chemical Society (ACS). 1975a–1989a. *Starting Salaries of Chemists and Chemical Engineers, 1975–1989* (individual reports). Washington, D.C.: ACS.

———. 1975b–1989b. *Salary Survey, 1975, 1980, 1985, 1989* (individual reports). Washington, D.C.: ACS.

American Chemical Society, Committee on Professional Training (ACS-CPT). 1990. "ACS Committee on Professional Training, 1989 Annual Report." *Chemical & Engineering News* 68 (April 30): 29–34.

American Council on Education HEATH Resource Center (ACE). 1989. *National*

Clearinghouse on Postsecondary Education for Individuals with Handicaps: Resource Directory, 1989. Washington, D.C.: ACE.

American Institute of Physics (AIP). 1988. *Physics in the High Schools.* New York: AIP (#R-340).

————. 1991. *Enrollments and Degrees.* New York: AIP (#R-151.28).

Anderson, James D. 1988. *The Education of Blacks in the South: 1860–1935.* Chapel Hill: University of North Carolina Press.

Association of American Medical Colleges (AAMC). 1990. *Bulletin* (February). Washington, D.C.: AAMC.

Astin, Alexander W., Eric L. Dey, William S. Korn, and Ellyne R. Riggs. 1991. *The American Freshman, Fall 1991.* Los Angeles: Cooperative Institutional Research Program of the American Council on Education and University of California-Los Angeles.

Astin, Alexander W., Kenneth C. Green, William S. Korn, and Marilynn Schalit. 1988. *The American Freshman: National Norms for Fall 1988.* Los Angeles: Higher Education Research Institute, Graduate School of Education.

Astin, Alexander W., William S. Korn, and Ellyne R. Riggs. 1993. *The American Freshman: National Norms for Fall 1993.* Los Angeles: Higher Education Research Institute, Graduate School of Education.

Astin, Helen S., and Diane E. Davis. 1985. "Research Productivity across Life and Career Cycles: Facilitators and Barriers for Women." Pp. 147–60 in Mary Frank Fox, ed., *Scholar Writing and Publishing: Issues, Problems, and Solutions.* Boulder, Colo.: Westview Press.

Atkinson, Richard C. 1990. "Supply and Demand for Scientists and Engineers: A National Crisis in the Making." *Science* 248: 425–32.

Bain, Joe S. 1956. *Barriers to New Competition: Their Character and Consequences in Manufacturing Industries.* Cambridge: Harvard University Press.

Baker, Joe G. 1989. "Biomedical and Behavioral Cohort Model: A Technical Paper." In National Research Council, *Biomedical and Behavioral Research Scientists: Their Training and Supply,* vol. 3, *Commissioned Papers.* Washington, D.C.: National Academy Press.

————. 1991. "Will There Be Enough Ph.D.s in the Year 2000?" Unpublished manuscript.

Benjamin, Marina. 1991. *Science and Sensibility: Gender and Scientific Enquiry, 1780–1945.* London: Basil Blackwell.

Bernstein, Aaron. 1988. "Where the Jobs Are Is Where the Skills Aren't." *Business Week* (September 19), pp. 104–8.

Blackwell, James E. 1981. *Mainstreaming Outsiders: The Production of Professionals.* Bayside, N.Y.: General Hall.

————. 1988. "Faculty Issues: The Impact on Minorities." *Review of Higher Education* 11 (4): 417–34.

Blalock, Hubert M. 1967. *Toward a Theory of Minority-Group Relations.* New York: John Wiley and Sons.

Blank, Rolf K., and Doreen Gruebel. 1993. *State Indicators of Science and Mathematics Education 1993: State and National Trends: New Indicators from the*

1991–92 School Year. Washington, D.C.: Council of Chief State School Officers.

Blum, Debra E. 1992. "Foreign Students Said to Get Aid Preference over U.S. Minorities." *Chronicle of Higher Education* (March 11), pp. A1, A30.

Borque, Mary Lyn, and Howard H. Garrison. 1991. *The Levels of Mathematics Achievement: Initial Performance Standards for the 1990 NAEP Mathematics Assessment*, vol. 1. Washington, D.C.: Aspen Systems for the National Assessment Governing Board.

Bowen, Howard, and Jack Schuster. 1986. *American Professors: A National Resource Imperiled*. New York: Oxford University Press.

Bowen, William G., and Neil Rudenstine. 1992. *In Pursuit of the Ph.D.* Princeton: Princeton University Press.

Bowen, William G., and Julie Ann Sosa. 1989. *Prospects for Faculty in the Arts and Sciences*. Princeton: Princeton University Press.

Boyer, Ernest. 1987. *Classification of Institutes of Higher Education*. Princeton: Carnegie Foundation for the Advancement of Teaching.

Brown, Shirley Vining, and Beatriz C. Clewell. 1991. *Building the Nation's Work Force from the Inside Out*. Norman, Okla.: Center for Research on Multi-Ethnic Education.

Bruffee, Kenneth A. 1992. "Science in a Postmodern World." *Change* 24 (September/October): 18–25.

Brush, Stephan. 1991. "Women in Science and Engineering." *American Scientist* 79: 404–19.

California Department of Education. 1992. "California Student Population: Grades K through 12." *EEO Bimonthly* (May/June), p. 8.

Campbell, Ernest Q. 1969. "Negroes, Education and the Southern States." *Social Forces* 47: 253–65.

Carson, Nancy, and Darryl Chubin. 1992. "Women in Science and Engineering: A Data Update." U.S. Congress Office of Technology Assessment Seminar. May 25.

Cartter, Allan M. 1976. *Ph.D.s and the Academic Labor Market*. New York: McGraw-Hill.

Center for the Assessment of Educational Progress. 1992a. *Learning Mathematics*. Report no. 22 CAEP-01. Princeton: Educational Testing Service.

———. 1992b. *Learning Science*. Report no. 22 CAEP-02. Princeton: Educational Testing Service.

Chubin, Darryl, and Elizabeth Robinson. 1992. "Human Resources for the Research Work Force: U.S. Indicators and Policy Choices." *Science and Public Policy* 19 (3): 181–85.

Clewell, Beatriz C., Beatrice T. Anderson, and Margaret E. Thorpe. 1992. *Breaking the Barriers: Helping Female and Minority Students Succeed in Mathematics and Science*. San Francisco: Jossey-Bass.

Clewell, Beatriz C., and Molly S. Ficklen. 1986. *Improving Minority Retention in Higher Education: A Search for Effective Institutional Practices*. Report no. RR-86–17. Princeton: Educational Testing Service.

Coates, Joseph F., Jennifer Jarratt, and John B. Mahaffie. 1990. *Future Work.* San Francisco: Jossey-Bass.

Cole, Jonathan R. 1979. *Fair Science: Women in the Scientific Community.* New York: Free Press.

———. 1987. "Women in Science." Pp. 359–75 in Douglas N. Jackson and J. Philippe Rushton, eds., *Scientific Excellence: Origins and Assessment.* Beverly Hills, Calif.: Sage.

Cole, Jonathan R., and Harriet Zuckerman. 1991. "Marriage, Motherhood and Research Performance in Science." Pp. 158–70 in Harriet Zuckerman, Jonathan R. Cole, and John T. Bruer, eds., *The Outer Circle: Women in the Scientific Community.* New York: Norton.

Cole, Stephen, and Robert Fiorentine. 1991. "Discrimination against Women in Science: The Confusion of Outcome with Process." Pp. 205–25 in Harriet Zuckerman, Jonathan R. Cole, and John T. Bruer, eds., *The Outer Circle: Women in the Scientific Community.* New York: Norton.

Committee on High School Biology Education, National Research Council. 1990. *Fulfilling the Promise: Biology Education in the Nation's Schools.* Washington, D.C.: National Academy Press.

Czujko, Roman, and David Bernstein. 1989. *Who Takes Science? A Report on Student Coursework in High School Science and Mathematics.* New York: American Institute of Physics.

Daniels, Jane C. 1990a. "Increasing the Number of Women in Engineering: The Role of Governors." In Karen Glass, ed., *Realizing the Potential of Women and Minorities in Engineering: Four Perspectives from the Field.* Washington, D.C.: National Governors Association.

———. 1990b. "A New W.E.P.A.N. for Women in Engineering." Pp. 217–22 in S. Z. Keith and P. Keith, eds., *Proceedings of the National Conference on Women in Mathematics and the Sciences.* St. Cloud, Minn.: St. Cloud State University.

DauffenBach, Robert C., and Jack Fiorito. 1983. *Projections of Supply of Scientists and Engineers to Meet Defense and Nondefense Requirements, 1981–1987.* Washington, D.C.: National Science Foundation.

de la Luz Reyes, Maria, and John J. Halcon. 1991. "Practices of the Academy for Chicano Academics." Pp. 167–86 in Phillip G. Altbach and Kofi Lomotey, eds., *The Racial Crisis in American Higher Education.* Albany: State University of New York Press.

Dertouzos, Michael L., Richard K. Lester, Robert M. Solow, and the MIT Commission on Industrial Productivity. 1989. *Made in America: Regaining the Productive Edge.* Cambridge: MIT Press.

Dix, Linda S., ed. 1987a. *Minorities: Their Underrepresentation and Career Differentials in Science and Engineering, Proceedings of a Workshop.* Washington, D.C.: National Academy Press.

———. 1987b. *Women: Their Underrepresentation and Career Differentials in Science and Engineering, Proceedings of a Workshop.* Washington, D.C.: National Academy Press.

Dossey, John A., Ina V. S. Mullis, Mary M. Lindquist, and Donald Chambers. 1988. *The Mathematics Report Card: Trends and Achievement Based on the 1986 National Assessment.* Princeton: Educational Testing Service.

Dowdall, Jean, and Ellen Boneparth. 1979. "Mentors in Academia: The Perceptions of Protege." Paper presented at the annual meeting of the American Sociological Association, Boston.

Eccles, Jacqueline S., and J. E. Jacobs. 1986. "Social Forces Shape Math Attitudes and Performance." *Signs* 11: 367–80.

Ehrenberg, Ronald G. 1991. "Academic Labor Supply." Pp. 143–258 in Charles T. Clotfelter, Ronald G. Ehrenberg, Malcom Getz, and John J. Siegfried, eds., *Economic Challenges in Higher Education.* Chicago: University of Chicago Press.

El-Khawas, Elaine. 1989. *Campus Trends, 1989.* American Council on Education Higher Education Panel Reports, no. 78.

Engineering Workforce Commission. 1993. *Engineering and Technology Degrees, 1993.* Washington, D.C.: American Association of Engineering Societies. Annual series, 1972–93.

———. 1994. *Engineering and Technology Enrollments, Fall 1993.* Washington, D.C.: American Association of Engineering Societies. Annual series, 1972–94.

Enna, Anne. 1993. "In Mitchell's Nineteenth-Century Vision, Women Find New Dreams." *Nantucket Inquirer and Mirror* (August 26), p. D1.

Epstein, Cynthia F. 1991. "Constraints on Excellence: Structural and Cultural Barriers to the Recognition and Demonstration of Achievement." Pp. 239–58 in Harriet Zuckerman, Jonathan R. Cole, and John T. Bruer, eds., *The Outer Circle: Women in the Scientific Community.* New York: Norton.

Etzkowitz, Henry. 1989. "Entrepreneurial Scientists in the Academy: A Case of the Transformation of Norms." *Social Problems* 36 (1): 14–29.

———. 1992. "Individual Investigators and Their Research Groups." *Minerva* 30: 28–50.

———. 1993. "Women Scientific Entrepreneurs: Overcoming the Marginalization of Women Scientists and Engineers in Industry and Academia." Paper presented at the Committee on Women in Science and Engineering, National Research Council, conference on "Women Scientists and Engineers Employed in Industry: Why So Few?" Irvine, Calif.

Etzkowitz, Henry, and Mary Frank Fox. 1991. "Women in Science and Engineering: Improving Participation and Performance in Doctoral Education." Funded proposal. National Science Foundation, Education and Human Resources Division.

Etzkowitz, Henry, Carol Kemelgor, Michael Neuschatz, and Brian Uzzi. 1992. "Athena Unbound: Barriers to Women in Academic Science and Engineering." *Science and Public Policy* 19 (3): 157–79.

Featherman, David L., and Robert M. Hauser. 1978. *Opportunity and Change.* New York: Academic.

Fechter, Alan. 1990. "Engineering Shortages and Shortfalls: Myths and Realities." *The Bridge* 20 (2): 16–20.

Federal Coordinating Council for Science, Engineering and Technology (FCCSET),

Committee on Education and Human Resources. 1992. "National Education Goals." In *By the Year 2000: First in the World*. Washington, D.C.: Executive Office of the President, Office of Science and Technology Policy.

Federal Security Agency. 1942. *National Survey of the Higher Education of Negroes*. Washington, D.C.: Government Printing Office.

Fleming, Jacqueline. 1984. *Blacks in College*. San Francisco: Jossey-Bass.

Fleming, John. 1990. *Educating America: Black Universities and Colleges— Strengths and Crises*. Washington, D.C.: Associated Publishers.

Fox, Mary Frank. 1989. "Women and Higher Education: Gender Differences in the Status of Students and Scholars." Pp. 217–35 in Jo Freeman, ed., *Women: A Feminist Perspective*. Mountain View, Calif.: Mayfield.

Fox, Mary Frank, and Sharlene Hesse-Biber. 1984. *Women at Work*. Mountain View, Calif.: Mayfield Publishing.

Freeman, Richard B. 1971. *Market for College-trained Manpower*. Cambridge: Harvard University Press.

———. 1976. "A Cobweb Model of the Supply and Starting Salary of New Engineers." *Industrial and Labor Relations Review* 29 (January): 236–48.

Gerson, Kathleen. 1985. *Hard Choices: How Women Decide about Work, Career and Motherhood*. Berkeley: University of California Press.

Goldman, Kevin. 1993. "Sexy SONY Ad Riles a Network of Women." *Wall Street Journal* (August 23), p. B3.

Goodstein, David L. 1993a. "Scientific Elites and Scientific Illiterates." *Engineering and Science* 56 (3): 23–31.

———. 1993b. "Scientific Ph.D. Problems." *American Scholar* 62 (2): 215–20.

Green, K. C. 1989. In Sigma Xi: *An Exploration of the Future and Quality of Undergraduate Education in Science, Mathematics and Engineering*. New Haven: Sigma Xi.

Hansen, W. Lee, H. B. Newburger, S. J. Schroeder, D. C. Stapleton, and D. J. Youngday. 1980. "Forecasting the Market for New Ph.D. Economists." *American Economic Review* 70 (1): 49–63.

Holden, Constance. 1989. "Wanted: 675,000 Future Scientists and Engineers." *Science* 244 (June 30): 1530–37.

Hsia, Jayjia. 1988. *Asian Americans in Higher Education and at Work*. Hillsdale, N.J.: Lawrence Erlbaum Associates.

Institute for Science, Space, and Technology. 1990. *Strengthening American Science and Technology: The Role of Minorities*. Baltimore: Career Communications Group.

Jackson, Kenneth W. 1991. "Black Faculty in Academia." Pp. 135–48 in Phillip G. Altbach and Kofi Lomotey, eds., *The Racial Crisis in American Higher Education*. Albany: State University of New York Press.

Jones, Dianne J., and Betty C. Watson. 1990. *High-Risk Students and Higher Education: Future Trends*. ASHE-ERIC Higher Education Report no. 3. Washington, D.C.: George Washington University, School of Education and Human Development.

Kanter, Rosabeth M. 1977. *Men and Women of the Corporation*. New York: Basic Books.

Keller, Evelyn. 1986. "How Gender Matters: Or Why It's So Hard for Us to Count Past Two." In Jan Harding, ed., *Perspectives on Gender and Science*. London: Falmer.

Kemelgor, Carol. 1989. "Research Groups in Molecular Biology: A Study of Normative Change in Academic Science." B.A. thesis, State University of New York, Purchase.

Keynes, Harvey. 1991. "Annual Report on UMTYMP: University of Minnesota Talented Youth in Mathematics Program." St. Paul: University of Minnesota Mathematics Department.

Landis, Raymond B. 1985. *Handbook on Improving the Retention and Graduation of Minorities in Engineering*. New York: National Action Council for Minorities in Engineering.

Lapointe, Archie E., Nancy A. Mead, and Gary W. Phillips. 1989. *A World of Differences: An International Assessment of Mathematics and Science*. Princeton: Educational Testing Service.

LeBold, William K. 1987. "Women in Engineering and Science: An Undergraduate Research Perspective." In Linda S. Dix, ed., *Women: Their Underrepresentation and Career Differentials in Science and Engineering, Proceedings of a Workshop*. Washington, D.C.: National Academy Press.

Lederman, Leon M. 1992. "The Advancement of Science." *Science* 256 (May 22): 1119–24.

Leggon, Cheryl. 1987. "Minority Underrepresentation in Science and Engineering Graduate Education and Careers: A Critique." In Linda S. Dix, ed., *Minorities: Their Underrepresentation and Career Differentials in Science and Engineering, Proceedings of a Workshop*. Washington, D.C.: National Academy Press.

———. 1991a. "Graduate Schools and Careers." Paper presented at a workshop on Minorities, Science, and Technology: An Agenda for Research and Action. Troy, N.Y., Rensselaer Polytechnic Institute.

———. 1991b. "Who Will Do Science?" Discussant, annual meeting of the American Association for the Advancement of Science, New Orleans.

Leong, Frederick T. 1991. "Career Development Attributes and Occupational Values of Asian American and White American College Students." *Career Development Quarterly* 39: 221–30.

Leslie, Larry R., and Ronald L. Oaxaca. 1993. "Scientist and Engineer Supply and Demand." Pp. 154–211 in John C. Smart, ed., *Higher Education: Handbook of Theory and Research*, Vol. 9. New York: Agathon Press.

Levin, Sharon G., and Paula E. Stephan. 1991. "Research Productivity over the Life Cycle: Evidence for American Scientists." *American Economic Review* (81): 114–32.

Long, Scott. 1990. "The Origins of Sex Differences in Science." *Social Forces* 68: 1297–1316.

Malcom, Shirley M. 1984. *Equity and Excellence: Compatible Goals*. Washington, D.C.: American Association for the Advancement of Science.

Marglin, S., and J. Schor, eds. 1989. *The End of the Golden Age*. New York: Oxford University Press.

Matthew, Christina. 1990. *Underrepresented Minorities and Women in Science, Mathematics, and Engineering: Problems and Issues for the 1990s.* Washington, D.C.: Library of Congress.

Matyas, Marsha Lakes. 1993. "Women and Disabled Scientists." Paper presented at the meeting of the American Sociological Association, Miami Beach.

Matyas, Marsha Lakes, and Linda S. Dix, eds. 1992. *Science and Engineering Programs: On Target for Women?* Washington, D.C.: National Academy Press.

Matyas, Marsha Lakes, and Shirley M. Malcom, eds. 1991. *Investing in Human Potential: Science and Engineering at the Crossroads.* Washington, D.C.: American Association for the Advancement of Science.

Max, Claire. 1982. "Career Paths for Women in Physics." Pp. 99–118 in Sheila Humphreys, ed., *Women and Minorities in Science: Strategies for Increasing Participation.* Boulder, Colo.: Westview.

McCuiston, Fred. 1939. *Graduate Instruction for Negroes.* Nashville: George Peabody College for Teachers.

Mcilwee, Judith, and J. Gregg Robinson. 1992. *Women in Engineering: Gender, Power, and Workplace Culture.* Albany: State University of New York Press.

Mercer, Joyce. 1992. "Broad Effort Aims to Replicate Florida Program Hailed for Helping Black Ph.D. Students." *Chronicle of Higher Education* 38 (32): A27, A29.

Merton, Robert K. 1973a. "The Normative Structure of Science." Pp. 267–80 in *The Sociology of Science: Theoretical and Empirical Investigations.* Chicago: University of Chicago Press.

————. 1973b. "Social Conflict over Social Styles of Sociological Work." Pp. 47–69 in *The Sociology of Science: Theoretical and Empirical Investigations.* Chicago: University of Chicago Press.

Mervis, Jeffrey. 1992. "Radcliffe President Lambastes Competitiveness in Research." *Scientist* 6 (2): 3.

Moen, Phyllis. 1988. "Women as a Human Resource." Washington, D.C.: National Science Foundation, Sociology Program, Division of Social and Economic Science.

Mokros, Janice R., Sumru Erkut, and Lynne Spichiger. 1981. "Mentoring and Being Mentored: Sex-Related Patterns among College Professors." Working paper no. 68, pp. 1–14. Wellesley: Wellesley College Center for Research on Women.

Morrison, Catherine. 1992. "The AT&T Bell Laboratories Cooperative Research Fellowship Program, 1972–1992: A Twenty-Year Review." New York: National Action Council for Minorities in Engineering.

Mullis, Ina V. S., John A. Dossey, Eugene H. Owen, and Gary W. Phillips. 1991. *The State of Mathematics Achievement.* Educational Testing Service for National Center for Education Statistics, report no. 21-ST-03. Washington, D.C.: Government Printing Office.

————. 1993. *NAEP 1992 Math Report Card for the Nation and the States.* Washington, D.C.: U.S. Department of Education, National Center for Education Statistics.

Mullis, Ina V. S., and Lynn B. Jenkins. 1988. *The Science Report Card: Trends and*

Achievement Based on the 1986 National Assessment. Princeton: Educational Testing Service.

National Action Council for Minorities in Engineering (NACME). 1991. *Research Letter* 2, no. 2 (December).

National Research Council (NRC). 1979. *Research Excellence through the Year 2000: The Importance of Maintaining a Flow of New Faculty into Academic Research.* Washington, D.C.: National Academy Press.

——. 1986. *The Impact of Defense Spending on Nondefense Engineering Labor Markets.* Washington, D.C.: National Academy Press.

——. 1988. *Foreign and Foreign-born Engineers in the United States: Infusing Talent, Raising Issues.* Washington, D.C.: National Academy Press.

——. 1989a. *Everybody Counts: A Report to the Nation on the Future of Mathematics Education.* Washington, D.C.: National Academy Press.

——. 1989b. *Summary Report 1988: Doctorate Recipients from United States Universities.* Washington, D.C.: National Academy Press.

——. 1990. *Summary Report 1989: Doctorate Recipients from United States Universities.* Washington, D.C.: National Academy Press.

——. 1991a. *Moving beyond Myths: Revitalizing Undergraduate Mathematics.* Washington, D.C.: National Academy Press.

——. 1991b. *Summary Report 1990: Doctorate Recipients from United States Universities.* Washington, D.C.: National Academy Press.

——. 1991c. *Women in Science and Engineering: Increasing Their Numbers in the 1990s.* Washington, D.C.: National Academy Press.

——. 1993a. *Summary Report 1991: Doctorate Recipients from United States Universities.* Washington, D.C.: National Academy Press.

——. 1993b. *Summary Report 1992: Doctorate Recipients from United States Universities.* Washington, D.C.: National Academy Press.

National Science Board (NSB). 1989. *Science and Engineering Indicators, 1989.* Washington, D.C.: Government Printing Office.

——. 1990. *A View from the National Science Board: The State of U.S. Science and Engineering.* Washington, D.C.: Government Printing Office.

——. 1991. *Science and Engineering Indicators,* 10th ed. Washington, D.C.: Government Printing Office.

National Science Foundation (NSF). 1979. *Projections of Science and Engineering Doctorate Supply and Utilization: 1982 and 1987.* Washington, D.C.: Government Printing Office.

——. 1984. *Women and Minorities in Science and Engineering.* Washington, D.C.: Government Printing Office.

——. 1989. "Future Scarcities of Scientists and Engineers: Problems and Solutions." Working draft (April 25).

——. 1990a. "Future Scarcities of Scientists and Engineers: Problems and Solutions." Working draft (summer).

——. 1990b. *Report of the National Science Foundation Task Force on Persons with Disabilities.* Washington, D.C.: Government Printing Office.

——. 1990c. *The State of Academic Science and Engineering.* Washington, D.C.: Government Printing Office.

————. 1990d. *Women and Minorities in Science and Engineering.* Washington, D.C.: Government Printing Office.

————. 1991. "Selected Data on Graduate Science/Engineering Students and Post-doctorates, Fall 1990." Early Release Statistics.

————. 1992a. "Selected Data on Graduate Science/Engineering Students and Postdoctorates, Fall 1991." NSF 92–335, Supplementary Data Releases.

————. 1992b. *Selected Data on Science and Engineering Doctorate Awards: 1991.* NSF 92–309. Washington, D.C.: Government Printing Office.

————. 1992c. "Women and Minorities in Science: An Update."

————. 1993. "Selected Data on Science and Engineering Doctorate Awards, 1992." NSF 93–315. Washington, D.C.: Government Printing Office.

Oakes, Jennie. 1990. *Lost Talent: The Underparticipation of Women, Minorities and Disabled Persons in Science.* Santa Monica, Calif.: Rand Corporation.

Oleson, Alexandra, and John Voss, eds. 1979. *The Organization of Knowledge in Modern America, 1860–1920.* Baltimore: Johns Hopkins University Press.

Pearson, Willie, Jr., and H. Kenneth Bechtel, eds. 1989. *Blacks, Science, and American Education.* New Brunswick: Rutgers University Press.

Pearson, Willie, Jr., and La Rue C. Pearson. 1985. "Baccalaureate Origins of Black American Scientists: A Cohort Analysis." *Journal of Negro Education* 54: 24–34.

Pelavin and Associates. 1990. *Changing the Odds: Factors Increasing Access to College.* Pub. no. 003969. New York: College Board.

Porter, Beverly. 1989. "Scientific Resources for the 1990s: Women, the Untapped Pool." Paper presented at the annual meeting of the American Association for the Advancement of Science.

Preer, J. 1982. *Lawyers v. Educators.* New York: Greenwood Press.

Quality Education for Minorities Project (QEM). 1990. *Education That Works: An Action Plan for the Education of Minorities.* Cambridge: MIT Press.

Radner, Roy, and Charlotte V. Kuh. 1978. "Preserving a Last Generation: Policies to Assure a Steady Flow of Young Scholars until the Year 2000." A report to the Carnegie Council on Policy Studies in Higher Education, October.

Radner, Roy, and Leonard S. Miller. 1975. *Demand and Supply in U.S. Higher Education.* New York: McGraw-Hill.

Reich, Robert B. 1991. *The Work of Nations: Preparing Ourselves for Twenty-first Century Capitalism.* New York: Knopf.

Rosenfeld, Rachel A. 1984. "Academic Career Mobility for Women and Men Psychologists." Pp. 89–127 in Violet B. Haas and Carolyn C. Perrucci, eds., *Women in Scientific and Engineering Professions.* Ann Arbor: University of Michigan Press.

Ruivo, Beatriz. 1987. "The Intellectual Labor Market in Developed and Developing Countries: Women's Representation in Scientific Research." *International Journal of Scientific Education* 9: 385–91.

Sayre, Anne. 1975. *Rosalind Franklin and DNA.* New York: Norton.

Scherer, Jacqueline, cited in Dianne J. Jones and Betty C. Watson. 1990. *High-Risk Students and Higher Education: Future Trends.* ASHE-ERIC Higher Education

Report no. 3. Washington, D.C.: George Washington University, School of Education and Human Development.

"School Noncompletion Rates by State." 1988. *Chronicle of Higher Education* (September 1).

Science. 1992. *Special Issue on Women in Science* 255: 1363–88.

Scott, Joan. 1990. "Disadvantage of Women by the Ordinary Processes of Science: The Case of Informal Collaboration." Pp. 316–28 in Marianne Ainley, ed., *Despite the Odds: Essays on Canadian Women and Science.* Montreal: Vehicle Press.

Shavlik, Dana L., Judith G. Touchton, and Carol R. Pearson. 1987. *The New Agenda of Women for Higher Education: A Report of the ACE Commission on Women in Higher Education.* Washington, D.C.: American Council on Education.

Sigelman, Lee, and Susan Welch. 1991. *Black Americans' Views of Racial Inequality: The Dream Deferred.* New York: Cambridge University Press.

Smith, Earl. 1991. "The Making of Black Scientists." *Black Issues in Higher Education* (March 14), p. 68.

Smith, Earl, and Willie Pearson, Jr. 1989. "Scientific Productivity among a Sample of Black and White Female Ph.D.s." *Journal of Social and Behavioral Sciences* 35: 153–74.

Society of Women Engineers. 1985. *A Profile of the Woman Engineer.* New York: Society of Women Engineers.

Solomon, Lewis C., and Tamara L. Wingard. 1991. "The Changing Demographics: Problems and Opportunities." Pp. 19–42 in Phillip G. Altbach and Kofi Lomotey, eds., *The Racial Crisis in American Higher Education.* Albany: State University of New York Press.

Sonnert, Gerhart. 1990. "Careers of Women and Men Postdoctoral Fellows in the Sciences." Paper presented at the annual meeting of the American Sociological Association, Washington, D.C.

Sposito, Gary. 1992. "Promoting Science and Engineering Careers in Academe." In Marsha L. Matyas and Linda S. Dix, eds., *Science and Engineering Programs: On Target for Women?* Washington, D.C.: National Academy Press.

Stampen, Jacob O., and Robert H. Fenske. 1988. "The Impact of Financial Aid on Ethnic Minorities." *Review of Higher Education* 11 (4): 337–54.

Talapessy, Lily, ed. 1993. *Women in Scientific and Technological Research in the European Community.* Brussels: Commission of the European Communities Directorate General for Science, Research and Development.

Tang, Joyce. 1991. "The Career Mobility of Asian American Engineers: Earnings, Career Status, Promotions, and Attrition." Ph.D. diss., University of Pennsylvania.

————. 1993. "Caucasians and Asians in Engineering: A Study in Occupational Mobility and Departure." Pp. 217–56 in S. B. Bacharach, ed., *Research in the Sociology of Organizations.* Greenwich, Conn.: JAI Press.

Thomas, Gail. 1984. *College Students and Factors Influencing Their Major Field Choice.* Atlanta: Southern Education Foundation.

————. 1989. "Black Science Majors in Colleges and Universities." Pp. 43–58 in Willie Pearson, Jr., and H. Kenneth Bechtel, eds., *Blacks, Science and American Education*. New Brunswick: Rutgers University Press.

————. 1990. "Black Students in U.S. Graduate and Professional Schools in the 1980s: A National and Institutional Assessment." Pp. 210–31 in N. M. Hidalgo, C. L. McDowell, and E. V. Siddle, eds., *Facing Racism in Education*. Cambridge: Harvard Education Review. Reprint series no. 21.

Tobias, Sheila. 1990. *They're Not Dumb, They're Different: Stalking the Second Tier*. Tucson, Ariz.: Research Corporation.

————. 1992. *Revitalizing Undergraduate Science: Why Some Things Work and Most Don't*. Tucson, Ariz.: Research Corporation.

Trent, William. 1984. "Equity Considerations in Higher Education: Racial Differences in Degree Attainment and Major Field from 1976 through 1981." *American Journal of Education* 41: 297–302.

Tuckman, Howard, Susan Coyle, and Y. Bae. 1990. *On Time to the Doctorate*. Washington, D.C.: National Academy Press.

Twombly, R. 1992. "Academic Researchers Pursue Survival As States Slash Budget Support for Science." *Scientist* 6 (11): 1, 6–7.

U.S. Bureau of the Census. 1990. "Projections of the Population of the United States by Age, Sex, and Race: 1988 to 2020." *Current Population Reports*. Washington, D.C.: Government Printing Office.

U.S. Congress, Office of Technology Assessment. 1988. *Educating Scientists and Engineers: From Grade School to Grad School*. OTA-SET-377. Washington, D.C.: Government Printing Office.

————. 1989a. *Elementary and Secondary Education for Science and Engineering: A Technical Memorandum*. Washington, D.C.: Government Printing Office.

————. 1989b. *Higher Education for Science and Engineering: A Background Paper*. OTA-BP-SET-52. Washington, D.C.: Government Printing Office.

————. 1990. *Worker Training: Competing in the New International Economy*. OTA-ITE-457. Washington, D.C.: Government Printing Office.

————. 1991. *Federally Funded Research: Decisions for a Decade*. OTA-SET-490. Washington, D.C.: Government Printing Office.

————. 1992. "Projecting Science and Engineering Personnel Requirements for the 1990s: How Good Are the Numbers?" Hearing before the Subcommittee on Investigations and Oversight of the Committee on Science, Space, and Technology.

U.S. Department of Education, National Center for Education Statistics (NCES). 1950–91. *Earned Degrees Conferred by U.S. Colleges and Universities*. Annual series, 1950–88. Data for 1989, 1990, 1991, and 1992 published in other documents (NCES *Digest* and Vetter, 1992, 1994).

————. 1985. *The Traditionally Black Institutions of Higher Education: 1869 to 1982*. Washington, D.C.: Government Printing Office.

————. 1988. *Digest of Education Statistics, 1988*. CS 88–600. Washington, D.C.: Government Printing Office.

————. 1989. *Digest of Education Statistics, 1989*. NCES 89–643. Washington, D.C.: Government Printing Office.

————. Unpublished. *Tabulations from the 1987 Survey of Recent College Grad-uates.*

U.S. Department of Health, Education, and Welfare. 1958. *Earned Degrees Con-ferred by Higher Education Institutions: 1956–57.* Washington, D.C.: Govern-ment Printing Office.

Vetter, Betty M., ed. 1989. *Professional Women and Minorities: A Manpower Data Resource Service.* 8th ed. Washington, D.C.: Commission on Profession-als in Science and Technology.

————. 1990. *Who Is in the Pipeline? Science, Math, Engineering Education.* Oc-casional Paper 90–3. Washington, D.C.: Commission on Professionals in Sci-ence and Technology.

————. 1992. *American Minorities in Science and Engineering.* Occasional Paper 92–1. Washington, D.C.: Commission on Professionals in Science and Tech-nology.

————. 1994. *Professional Women and Minorities: A Total Human Resource Data Compendium.* 11th ed. Washington, D.C.: Commission on Professionals in Science and Technology.

Watson, Bernard. 1972. "Blacks in Higher Education: A Position Paper." Paper presented to the First National Congress of Black Professionals in Higher Educa-tion, Austin, Tex.

Weis, Lois. 1987. "Academic Women in Science, 1977–1984." *Academe* (January/February), pp. 43–47.

Weiss, Iris. 1988. *1985–1986 National Survey of Science and Mathematics Educa-tion.* Chapel Hill, N.C.: Research Triangle Institute.

————. 1989. *Science and Mathematics Education Briefing Book.* Chapel Hill, N.C.: Horizon Research.

Westat, Inc. 1993. *The 1990 High School Transcript Study Tabulations: Compara-tive Data on Credits Earned and Demographics for 1990, 1987 and 1982 High School Graduates.* Washington, D.C.: U.S. Department of Education, National Center for Education Statistics.

Zuckerman, Harriet, Jonathan Cole, and John Bruer, eds. 1991. *The Outer Circle: Women in the Scientific Community.* New York: Norton.

Zuniga, Robin Etter. 1991. *The Road to College: Educational Progress by Race and Ethnicity.* Boulder, Colo.: Western Interstate Commission for Higher Edu-cation.

Contributors

Henry Etzkowitz is Associate Professor of Sociology at the State University of New York at Purchase and Research Professor at the Center for Science and Technology Policy, Rensselaer Polytechnic Institute. He is the founding chair of the Section on Science, Knowledge and Technology in the American Sociological Association. He is co-principal investigator (with Mary Frank Fox) of an NSF-sponsored study of "Women in Science and Engineering: Improving Participation and Performance in Doctoral Programs."

Alan Fechter is Executive Director of the Office of Scientific and Engineering Personnel at the National Research Council. Educated at CCNY and the University of Chicago, he has been engaged for the major part of his career in policy studies. His research on enlistment behavior was an important input to the implementation of policies to eliminate the draft. His evaluation of public employment programs was a critical part of the debate on the implementation of such programs to reduce the cyclical unemployment cycle. In 1978, he accepted a position at the National Science Foundation, where he was head of the Scientific and Technical Personnel Studies Section, Division of Science Resources Studies. During his tenure, he confronted such topics as the expected impact of the defense buildup on scientific and technical personnel, the quality of the scientific and technical work force, and the role of women and minorities in this work force. He has been affiliated with the National Research Council since 1983. His recent analysis and critique of estimates of future shortfalls of scientists and engineers fueled a strong debate about the validity of such estimates. He has been a member of the Committee on the Status of Women in the Economics Profession and is a member of the Commission on Professionals in Science and Technology. He has served on advisory boards for the National Center for Educational Statistics, American Chemical Society, and American Society for Engineering Education.

John Hill is an analyst with the U.S. Department of Education. His main areas of interest are the sociology of education and education financing. A graduate of the University of Maryland College Park, he has examined issues related to the relationship of policy affecting colleges and universities and the underrepresented groups of students they serve.

Carol Kemelgor, M.S.W., C.S.W., is a graduate of New York University. In addition to her clinical practice, she has been research associate on several women in science studies with a particular interest in the psychodynamics of groups and personality development.

Cheryl B. Leggon is Associate Professor of Sociology at Wake Forest University. Before joining the Wake Forest University faculty in 1993, she was a Staff Officer in the Studies and Surveys Unit of the Office of Scientific and Engineering Personnel at the National Research Council and an Adjunct Associate Professor of Sociology at Georgetown University. She earned her Ph.D. in sociology from the University of Chicago, and she has held postdoctoral fellowships at the University of Chicago and at the Center for Advanced Study in the Behavioral Sciences at Stanford University. Her research focuses on human resource issues in science and technology.

Shirley M. Malcom is a member of the National Science Board and Head of the Directorate for Education and Human Resources Programs of the American Association for the Advancement of Science (AAAS). The directorate includes AAAS programs in education, activities for underrepresented groups, and public understanding of science and technology. She received her doctorate in ecology from the Pennsylvania State University. Currently, she serves on the boards of the American Museum of Natural History, Scientists' Institute for Public Information, and Carnegie Corporation of New York.

Marsha Lakes Matyas is the Education Officer for the American Physiological Society (APS). Formerly, she was Project Director in the Directorate for Education and Human Resources Programs at the American Association for the Advancement of Science (AAAS). Her research fields include factors affecting science and engineering interests and participation rates among women and minorities at both the precollege and undergraduate levels. She earned her master's degree in cell biology and her doctorate in science education at Purdue University. At the APS, she directs a number of education programs, including a summer research experience program for high school teachers and a mentoring program for graduate and postdoctoral women in physiology.

Michael Neuschatz is Senior Research Associate with the Employment and Education Statistics Division of the American Institute of Physics in College Park, Maryland. He earned a Ph.D. in sociology from the University of Colorado, and he has written extensively on the subject of science education.

Willie Pearson, Jr., is Professor of Sociology at Wake Forest University. His main fields of interest are the sociology of science and the sociology of the family. He has published in various scholarly journals and is the author of *Black Scientists, White Society, and Colorless Science* (1985) and co-editor (with H. K. Bechtel) of *Blacks, Science, and American Education* (1989). He received his doctorate from Southern Illinois University at Carbondale in 1981 and is a former Congressional

Science and Engineering Fellow. Currently, he is working on books on African Americans in engineering and the careers of African American Ph.D. chemists.

Terrence Russell is Executive Director of the Association for Institutional Research (AIR), an international association of administrators and faculty devoted to management research, policy analysis, and planning in higher education. He received his doctorate from Southern Illinois University at Carbondale in 1979. He is also Adjunct Associate Professor of Higher Education at Florida State University. Before coming to AIR in 1991, he was Manager of Professional Services for the American Chemical Society.

Earl Smith is Professor and Dean, Division of Social Sciences at Pacific Lutheran University in Tacoma, Washington. He received his Ph.D. from the University of Connecticut at Storrs. His major research interests are in the areas of race relations, the sociology of sport, urban sociology, and the sociology of science. He is currently studying the history of African Americans in engineering.

Joyce Tang is Assistant Professor of Sociology at Queens College in New York City. She received her doctorate from the University of Pennsylvania in 1991. Her recent papers on scientists and engineers appear in *Research in the Sociology of Organizations* (1993), *Sociological Quarterly* (1993), and *Research in Social Stratification and Mobility* (1993). Her research focuses on the labor market experiences of minorities and women in professional occupations and on stratification processes in science.

William T. Trent is Professor of Educational Policy Studies and Sociology at the University of Illinois at Urbana-Champaign. He received his Ph.D. in sociology from the University of North Carolina at Chapel Hill. His current research interests include equity issues in higher education, the desegregated schooling experience, race, class, and cultural implications for educational attainment. He is currently associate editor of the *Sociological Quarterly*.

Brian Uzzi is Assistant Professor at the School of Management, Northwestern University. His dissertation examines how the structure and substance of relationships among firms in networks affect organizational decline processes. He holds an M.S. in organizational behavior from Carnegie-Mellon University.

Betty M. Vetter is the Executive Director of the Commission on Professionals in Science and Technology (formerly the Scientific Manpower Commission), in Washington, D.C. She held academic appointments in California and in several universities in the Washington, D.C., area prior to her appointment to the Commission in 1963. She is editor of the periodical *Scientific, Engineering, Technical Manpower Comments*; and author of numerous published reports, book chapters, and articles on some phase of production or utilization of scientists and engineers.

Library of Congress Cataloging-in-Publication Data

Who will do science? : educating the next generation / edited by Willie Pearson, Jr., and
   Alan Fechter.
     p.   cm.
   Includes bibliographical references.
   ISBN 0-8018-4857-1 (acid-free paper)
     1. Science and state—United States. 2. Engineering and state—United States.
  3. Education and state—United States. 4. Education—Demographic aspects—
United States. 5. Minorities in science—United States. I. Pearson, Willie, 1945–
II. Fechter, Alan.
Q127.U6W48 1994
338.97306—dc20   94-9005